D0784143

The
SPIRIT OF GOLF

This book is dedicated to the juniors of golf, those ambitious, aspiring,

incredibly dedicated, and untiring boys and girls upon whose shoulders the future

quality, integrity, and character of the game rests.

The ROLEX Player of the Year Award
presented to the outstanding junior boy in
American Junior Golf Association events.
Bronze by Ray Ellis

1. Panorama at Turnberry, *Scotland*

The
SPIRIT OF GOLF

RAY ELLIS / BEN WRIGHT

INTRODUCTION BY HERBERT WARREN WIND

LONGSTREET PRESS

Published by
LONGSTREET PRESS, INC.
A subsidiary of Cox Newspapers, Inc.
2140 Newmarket Parkway
Suite 118
Marietta, GA 30067

Paintings copyright © 1992 by Ray Ellis
Narrative copyright © 1992 by Ben Wright
Foreword copyright © 1992 by Herbert Warren Wind
Photographs © 1992 by John deGarmo

All rights reserved. No part of this book may be reproduced in any form or by any means without
the prior written permission of the Publisher, excepting brief quotations used in connection with
reviews, written specifically for inclusion in a magazine or newspaper.

1st paperback printing 1996

Library of Congress Catalog Card Number: 92-71792

ISBN 1-56352-275-6

The text was set in Goudy Oldstyle.
Jacket and book design by Jill Dible.
Ektachromes of paintings by Ross Meurer.

2. The Caddy

The Inspiration

This gallery of golf art and prose was inspired partially by my agonies and ecstasies around the world of golf . . . but more importantly by my golfing peers of many years. Four of them rush to mind. They are quite different as personalities yet so alike in their respect and enthusiasm for the game. And what gentlemen they are!

Walter Pedersen was my god-father. He also fathered Pedersen golf clubs. One of the game's great innovators, he put metal woods on the market in 1926. He also developed the first graded shafts and the first color-coordinated clubs — all of this before World War II. Occasionally, and then only for short moments, he could be monumentally crabby on the golf course, but at all other times his manner was encouraging and ingenuous.

Bob Kiersky is the kind of man most of us would like to be. He has great pride, great humility, and is a great competitor. He took up golf at age 35, and at 54 he won the Long Island Amateur by winning the semis and finals on the same day against two young men whose aggregate age didn't equal his. He also won the U.S. Seniors. He is a true golfer-gentleman.

Mike Krak was a tour pro, then a club professional, but always a great father, husband, and friend. No one that I've known in golf ever embraced the game more nor tried harder to help others to play better. If you wanted to learn and would work at it, Mike was there. Never mind the dollars.

Jim Benham, whom I've worked with in business and played golf with and against so many times, is a man no one ever lost to; the camaraderie and sheer pleasure of the occasion made everyone a winner.

The warmth that results from having played and talked about the game with these men, and so many others, is truly what kindled *The Spirit of Golf.*

— John deGarmo

Dedication

The great game of golf has been a part of my life for close to 70 years. I grew up in Glenside, Pennsylvania, next to a farm turned into a nine-hole course; I harbor wonderful memories of learning to play with my wood-shafted clubs. Given the fact that I started playing at such a young age, my handicap should be substantially lower. But I have had to accept the fact that I paint golf much better than I play it.

In all my travels around this country and abroad, some of the most beautiful vistas and interesting landscapes I have seen have been on or around golf courses. When John deGarmo came to me with the idea for *The Spirit of Golf,* I jumped at the chance to lessen my frustration with my scores and hopefully leave something of beauty and merit to this great and timeless game.

I admire and am in awe of the touring pros, the scratch golfers, and even the single-digit handicappers. But I am among the many millions who are elated to break a hundred now and then, and I proudly display my only hole-in-one ball in the bookcase. One thing is certain — we never lose our love of the game or our optimism for it.

My hope is that this book will give as much pleasure to the reader and the viewer as it did to those of us who produced it.

— Ray Ellis

To my brother-in-law, Bill Dando; my brother, Dick Ellis; and all of those with whom I have spent happy hours on the golf course.

When I was a spindly youth, my father would drop me off at the South Bedfordshire Golf Club on his way to work at the Skefko Ball Bearing Company before eight o'clock every morning of the school holidays, come rain mostly, come shine occasionally.

I would play 54 holes daily with anybody kind enough to tolerate me, more often alone, when I was able to indulge my fantasies. Ben Hogan, my idol, never got the better of me. I always carried my tattered Sunday bag full of ill-assorted and scruffy weapons. My father would collect me, often soaking wet as I was, and take me home to supper, whereupon I would regale my mother with tall tales of all the 20-footers that had got away that day. Now I'm glad to get home to bore my dear wife Kitty with a minute description of the one 10-footer I holed that day. How times change.

I am in awe of Ray Ellis's magnificent paintings herein, and I only hope that my disconnected jottings, some original, others culled from a 38-year career as a journalist, will be even half as interesting as are Ray's illustrations in oil and watercolors.

I am deeply touched and honored that Herbert Warren Wind, the finest golf writer this country has ever produced, consented to write an Introduction to our book. And I am tickled pink that John deGarmo asked me to supply the words to go alongside Ray's beautiful brush work.

— Ben Wright

To my mother, who made her first visit to my American home in May 1992, on the eve of her 86th birthday, and to my wife Kitty and my daughter Margaret, aged 10, for allowing me so much time on the golf course with nary a word of complaint.

3. To the Tee, *Winged Foot, Mamaroneck, New York*

Introduction

In the early years of this century, golf underwent two significant changes that made it a far better game. In 1902 the old gutta percha ball was replaced by the rubber-cored ball which was less capricious and flew straighter and farther. In the 1930s, the old hickory-shafted clubs gave way to steel-shafted clubs that were both more uniform and more powerful. Minor wrinkles were introduced down through the decades, but in the 1980s a decided change took place. Golf-ball manufacturers began to bring out a new species (with thinner covers and higher compression) that went farther than golf balls had ever gone before, especially when they were struck by golfers using the new ultra-modern clubs whose shafts and heads were made of graphite and other such esoteric metals and compounds. Today it is not at all unusual for the big hitters to wallop their tee shots over three hundred yards, and, in addition, to find their ball lying in perfect position, since the new balls are apparently constructed to seek the center of the fairway. One would think that the United States Golf Association, the official governing body of game in this country, would have spoken up before now and tempered with experience and sound judgment some of the excesses of contemporary golf.

We certainly inhabit a strange new world of golf today. Over the last fifteen years, with the game booming as never before, some of the shrewdest and most imaginative international entrepreneurs decided that this was the ideal time to invest in grandiose new golf complexes in relatively untouched areas around the globe as the starting point for huge land-development programs. Here at home there are as many as three or four fairly meaningful tournaments scheduled each week, and sometimes all of them are televised nationally. A good many of these telecasts are painfully superficial, but it is no longer true that the four major championships are the only televised golf worth watching. We all learned this in the early autumn of 1991 when the European Ryder Cup team met the United States team at the Ocean Course on Kiawah Island in South Carolina. On those three days all of us found that we couldn't leave the television set for even a few minutes, so tightly gripped were we by how deeply the players on both teams, the famous veterans and the comparatively unknown young men alike, cared about winning their individual matches and the team match. I wonder if we will ever experience that feeling again.

Some of the new-to-the-game zealots are convinced that the present world of golf is a vast improvement on the game's earlier eras. On the other hand, most of the golfers I know are not exactly delighted about the game's lack of a sound foundation. Golfers of my era, who were introduced to golf in the period between the two world wars, tend to be unhappy about the present state of affairs. We think the game that Nelson and Snead and Hogan and Palmer and Nicklaus played was better than the one we have today. What style and discipline the earlier champions had! I can still see Hogan in my mind's eye. Before playing an approach to a green, he walks 18 yards or so beyond his ball, his eyes fixed on the distant pin; he folds his arms and narrows his eyes as he studies the position of the pin and gets the feel of the air; satisfied that he has the information he needs, he walks with that same set expression back to his ball, quickly selects the iron he wants, gets the feel of the club in his hands and fingers, makes a little half-swing to refresh his feel of the club, carefully settles into his stance, and, after a brief waggle, hits the ball dead on the line to the flag. Whether his approach sits down seven feet from the cup or 25 undistinguished feet away, his deeply tanned face remains expressionless beneath his white cap as he walks to the green.

This reverie is not meant to demean in any way the skills and the styles of

4. Off the 10th tee, *Royal Troon, Scotland*

wonderful golfers like Tom Watson and Seve Ballesteros, who broke through in the major championships in the 1970s, and of the more recent heroes who have come to the forefront in the past decade. For instance, have any of us ever seen finer golf played over four rounds than Nick Faldo summoned in winning his two Masters and the second of his two British Opens? The standard of the golf produced under immense pressure in major events during the last few years by Hale Irwin, Ian Woosnam, Ian Baker-Finch, and Fred Couples has been absolutely dazzling. Today's champions are playing a quite different game than Hogan and his contemporaries did. The ball travels so far these days that on most par fours on first-rate courses they are left with relatively short pitches to the green. Another thing: with the new and improved versions of the sand wedge in their bags, bunkers nowadays hold no terror for them.

The recent changes in the fabric of the game are one of the aspects of contemporary golf that prompted John deGarmo to undertake *The Spirit of Golf*. A top-drawer New York advertising man, deGarmo has been a scratch golfer since his early twenties. Down through the years he has played and photographed the outstanding courses in this country and in Scotland, England, Wales, and Ireland. The key man in the team he put together in this book is Ray Ellis, the brilliant painter who is perhaps best known for his work on three huge books about coastwise sailing on the Atlantic and Pacific which he did in collaboration with Walter Cronkite. The text for this book was provided by Ben Wright, the gifted English journalist, who has gained a devoted following in this country as the anchorman on the team of commentators that handles the golf telecasts on the CBS network.

As deGarmo studied the current golf scene, he felt the time had come to introduce today's golfers to the game's formative years in Scotland and its eventual spread throughout the British Isles and around the world. Golf historians are of the opinion that a rudimentary form of golf was played in Scotland as early as the twelfth century. The game grew in fits and starts. In 1744, the first modern golf club, the Honourable Company of Edinburgh Golfers, was founded by a select group of enthusiasts who played the game on the links of Leith. The club moved to Musselburgh, some seven miles to the east in 1831, and sixty years later it moved east again to its present home, the beautiful links of Muirfield, on the southern shore of the Firth of Forth. The British Open championship — in Britain it is called The Open — is held at Muirfield every six years or so.

The world's second-oldest golf club, the Society of St. Andrews Golfers, was established on May 14, 1754, by "twenty-two noblemen and gentlemen" in the old gray town of St. Andrews which overlooks a handsome stretch of linksland near the eastern tip of the peninsula of Fife. (As the crow flies, St. Andrews is only 30 miles from Edinburgh.) In 1836, thanks to the dazzling footwork of Major Murray Belshes of Buttergash, a member of St. Andrews who was a born public relations man, King William IV of England agreed to become the club's patron and authorized the club to style itself the Royal and Ancient Golf Club of St. Andrews. The R and A, as it has come to be called, is

5. The Bell, *Prestwick, Scotland*

the official governing body for golf throughout the world with the exception of the United States, where the USGA performs those duties and services. In 1848, golf became a much better game and a far more popular one when the old feather-stuffed ball was replaced by a new ball made of gutta percha, a plastic gum found in Malaya. The "gutty" flew much farther than the old "feathery," it was cheaper to make, and it lasted a good deal longer. It revolutionized golf and made it much more popular. The British Open was first held at Prestwick on the west coast of Scotland in 1860. The elite field played three rounds over the 12-

6. Lining Up at Portmarnock, *Dublin, Ireland*

hole course in one day. In 1870 "Young Tom" Morris, the game's first great player, won the third of his four consecutive Opens with a total of 149. That averages out to 74 1/2 strokes per 18 holes, and it was never equalled in the Open in the nineteenth century.

The gutta percha ball hastened the growth of golf south of the Scottish border. The first English golf club, Westward Ho!, or Royal North Devon, was established in 1864. It was followed a year later by Royal Wimbledon, on the edge of London, and in 1869 by Royal Liverpool on the links of Hoylake. (In 1885, Royal Liverpool became the founding father of the British Amateur Championship.) In the last 30 years of the century, the game spread around the world. Royal Montreal, the first permanent golf club in North America, was founded in 1873, and the St. Andrews Golf Club, the first permanent American golf club, came into being in Yonkers, New York, in December 1888. By that time the game was also beginning to become a part of the lives of the well-to-do

on the European continent and was starting to grow roots in India, South Africa, Australia, New Zealand, and other outposts of the British Empire.

At the turn of the century, an event of immeasurable significance took place in our country: Coburn Haskell, a resident of Cleveland who was displeased with the gutta percha ball, invented, with the assistance of a friend who worked for the Goodrich Rubber Company, the rubber-cored ball. He did this by winding rubber strippings tightly around a solid rubber core and covering the sphere with a sheath of gutta percha. Harry Vardon, the most talented British golfer since "Young Tom" Morris, switched to the new ball in 1903. (Incidentally, in 1913 when Vardon and Ted Ray, his huge fellow-countryman, toured our country, they lost the United States Open in a historic three-way playoff at The Country Club in Brookline, Massachusetts, to Francis Ouimet, an all but unknown twenty-year-old amateur who had learned the game caddying at The Country Club.) Walter Hagen, the first impressive professional golfer who was born and raised in our country, played the slightly heavier British version of the rubber-cored ball when he went to England in 1920 to take a crack at the British Open, which was held at Deal that year. He found he could not control his customary high-parabola shots in the heavy winds off the English Channel. Since the British Open is always held on seaside courses, Hagen realized that he had to depart from the style of play that had made him the premier shotmaker in the United States. After learning how to keep the ball low beneath the wind, he finished sixth in the 1921 British Open at St. Andrews. In 1922 he broke through at Sandwich, which is practically next door to Deal. When he set off on his last round, in relatively balmy weather, Hagen was a stroke behind the leader, and a solid 72 saw him through. He won the championship a second time in 1924 with a thrilling dash down the last five holes at Hoylake. He won it a third time in 1928 when the championship was again staged at Sandwich, and in 1929 he went out in glory when he won his fourth and final British Open at Muirfield. On the third day, when

7. Hell Bunker at St. Andrews, *Scotland. Where it all started.*

the last two rounds were played in a punishing storm off the sea, Hagen switched to a deep-faced driver with a minimum of loft, and, according to Henry Longhurst, did not hit a drive more than 20 feet high. Most of the contending players could not cope with the wild conditions, but Hagen calmly put together a pair of 75s and finished six shots ahead of the nearest man.

In three of the years that Hagen did not win the British Open in the 1920s, Bobby Jones did — in 1926 at Lytham St. Annes, in 1927 at St. Andrews, and in 1930 at Hoylake. Jones had set up the possibility of a Grand Slam of the four major championships in 1930 when he won the British Amateur for the first time with a series of dramatic dashes down the stretch. Hoylake was the venue of the British Open that year. Tired and edgy, Jones never found his best form, but he held on grimly and at length finished two strokes ahead of Macdonald Smith and Leo Diegel. (Along with Harry Cooper, Diegel and Mac Smith are perhaps the finest golfers who never won a major championship.) Shortly after returning home, Jones teed it up in the U.S. Open, which was played at Interlachen, in Minneapolis, in July. He moved into the lead with a 68 on the third round, and down the stretch he staved off another bid by Mac Smith. Jones at length completed his sweep of the "impregnable quadrilateral" the last week in September when he simply marched through the field in the U.S. Amateur at Merion, that lovely course on the edge of Philadelphia.

The achievements of Hagen and Jones changed the world of golf. During the late 1920s and early 1930s, it became evident that the up-and-coming American professionals had discovered new methods of shotmaking that were clearly superior to those favored by the best British golfers of that day. The different climate and course conditions in our country accounted for this. Long hours on the practice tee helped the ambitious young men to master the split-second timing that the pronounced inside-out swing required and the added distance and accuracy they were after. Wise young Henry Cotton, who had come to this country from England to see what was going on, quickly understood the new techniques

our young professionals were working on, and he incorporated many of them into his sound, weatherproof game. He adopted the American method of playing bunker shots. He looked into the new wrinkles in American putting, but in the end he stayed with his own style. No other foreign golfer understood as clearly as Cotton how farsighted our young pros were in devising the modern practice tee and the modern practice green.

Following in the footsteps of Hagen and Sarazen, Jones and Lawson Little (who won both the British Amateur and the U.S. Amateur in 1934 and 1935), American golfers of all ages and degrees of skill began to descend on the British Isles in large numbers during the summer months. They had heard about the rugged courses on which the Open was held, and they were eager to see if linksland golf was all it was cracked up to be. Many of them headed for St. Andrews and found that the Old Course far surpassed their expectations. They took side-trips to Carnoustie and found that some days the piercing winds off the North Sea were more than they could handle. It was no easy matter for touring Americans to get to play Muirfield, but those who did usually found that the course exceeded their expectations in every respect. For a change of pace they could drive inland to Gleneagles with its splendid men's course, ladies' course, and putting course in addition to its comfortable hotel. (The best smoked salmon in the world was available in the Salle de Soleil.) Scotland is a surprisingly small country, and in a couple of hours visiting golfers can drive from the east coast to the west coat and see if they can bring Prestwick, Troon, Western Gailes, et al. to their knees. It's a rare place, Scotland. The people are so real and so accommodating that travelers keep returning there all their lives.

In the 20-year interval between the two world wars, one of the few things the British and Irish golf fans could cheer about was Cotton's play in the British Open. He won it for the first time at Sandwich in 1934, after starting with rounds of 67 and 65, fantastic scores in those days. In 1937, he again led

8. The Spectacles, *Carnoustie, Scotland, 14th hole*

9. Cart Reflections, *Pine Lakes,*
Myrtle Beach, South Carolina

the way in the British Open, which was played in bad weather at Carnoustie. That year the Ryder Cup was held in Britain. Our team won it handily, but none of our pros was in contention in the British Open. (Eleven years later, in 1948, Cotton, at 41, captured the championship for the third and last time. He dashed into the lead with a 66 on the third round and ultimately won by five strokes.) There was little else for the home folks to cheer about.

When the biennial Ryder Cup matches had gotten underway in 1927, the British and Irish team had started off well, taking the first two matches played at home, but after that the Americans held the upper hand. The Walker Cup series between the American and British amateurs had started in 1922 at the first monumental American course, the National Golf Links in Southampton, New York. Bernard Darwin, far and away the best of all golf writers, ended up captaining the British team and won his singles. The United States won the match, 8-4. The American amateurs went on to sweep the next eight Walker Cup matches, but in 1938 at St. Andrews the British and Irish team produced some inspired golf down the stretch on the second and last day and broke through at last, 7-4. (No half points were awarded then in halved matches.) The women amateurs got into the act in 1932. The American team won three of the four matches that were played before the outbreak of the Second World War and tied the other.

When national and international golf was resumed in 1946, Sam Snead flew across the Atlantic a day or two before the British Open got underway at St. Andrews. He carried it off with some resolute golf on the last nine holes and flew home almost immediately. Sam had finished four strokes ahead of Arthur D'Arcy "Bobby" Locke, the heavy-set, easy-going South African who played every shot with draw, i.e. an educated hook. This applied to his putting stroke as well, and he was one of the best putters of all times. Locke won the British Open in 1949, 1951, 1952, and 1957 at Sandwich, Troon, Lytham St. Annes, and St. Andrews respectively. Peter Thomson then came to the fore. Congenial and highly intel-

ligent, this young man from Melbourne, Australia, led the way in the British Open in 1954, 1955, 1956, 1958, and once again in 1965. In 1953, when neither Locke nor Thomson won the British, an American did — Ben Hogan. Ben had broken through in our Open championship in 1948 at Riviera on the edge of Los Angeles. After a miraculous recovery from a near-fatal automobile accident, he won our Open at Merion in 1950 and at Oakland Hills, near Detroit, in 1951. In 1953, when Ben raised the quality of his shotmaking to a discernibly higher level in winning his third Masters and his fourth U.S. Open, at Oakmont, the cry went up that it would be historically wrong if Ben, who had never played in the British Open, did not fly over to Scotland that summer, when the championship would be held at Carnoustie, and see how well he could handle the vicissitudes of playing a long seaside links in cold, heavy, and swirling winds. When friends found him in a comfortable apartment in Dundee some eight miles from the course, he flew to Britain eleven days before the start of the championship and spent one long day after another getting to know the course and adjusting his game to it. He found out early on that he was hurting his hands and wrists when he drove his clubhead into the hard ground, and he decided to make contact with the ball a bit more cleanly than he normally did. As Sir Guy Campbell remarked, "He ended up taking the ball exactly like the great Scottish golfers had done years and years before." In the championship — the weather was cold and windy, and there was a chilly rain from time to time — Ben put together four practically errorless rounds of 73, 71, 70, and 68 for a total of 282. That was four strokes lower than the score posted by the four men who tied for second.

In the years following the close of the Second World War, there was such an increase in the number of golf tournaments played around the world that it was hard to keep up with them. People were eager to enjoy themselves, and the long-distance airplane made travel much easier. In 1946, Mildred "Babe" Didrikson Zaharias, of Beaumont, Texas — she had come to fame as a track-and-field star in the 1932 Olympic Games — won the U.S. Women's Amateur. The

9

following year, at Gullane in Scotland, she became the first American to carry off the British Ladies' Championship. She hit the ball yards farther than anyone else in the field, played her irons crisply, and displayed a beautiful touch on and around the greens. She turned professional on returning home and was a key figure, along with Patty Berg, Louise Suggs, Betty Jameson, and other former amateur stars, in founding the Ladies Professional Golf Association and the LPGA Tour. Babe died in 1956 from cancer, and she has been deeply missed.

In leading the PGA Tour in prize money in 1947, Jimmy Demaret collected less than $28,000 — not a shabby figure in those days — but large, appreciative crowds were turning out and a golden future was in prospect for professional golf. John J. Hopkins, the chairman of the board of General Dynamics, was of the opinion that golf could do a great deal to achieve a better understanding among nations. To achieve this, he founded the International Golf Association. In the summer of 1953, two professional golfers from seven countries met in Montreal and played in the IGA's first tournament for the Canada Cup. The following year teams from 25 countries were on hand at Montreal, and so it went. In time the Canada Cup came to be called the World Cup and was played in a different country each year. In 1957, Snead and Hogan represented the United States when the event was held on the West Course of the Wentworth Golf Club, the notorious "Burma Road," to the west of London. The following year, when the tournament was held on the superlative East Course of the Kasumigaseki Country Club in Japan, it was a smash: the Japanese team of Torakichi "Pete" Nakamura and Koichi Ono outplayed the American team of Snead and Demaret on the final round and won going away. That was the day when the Japanese really became mad about golf.

In the spring of 1958, the representatives of the national golf associations of 35 countries met in Washington, D.C., established the World Amateur Golf Council, and arranged for the first World Amateur Team Championship for the Eisenhower Trophy to be played that October in St. Andrews. Although he had not been in good health for some time, Bob Jones, as he now preferred to be

called, was so delighted by the whole concept that he agreed to act as captain of the four-man American team. The high point of the gala week in St. Andrews, as it turned out, came on the night when Jones was formally made a Freeman of the Burgh of St. Andrews. The last American to be so honored was Benjamin Franklin. The hall was jammed to the rafters that night by some two thousand lifelong golfers, most of them townspeople. The town clerk read the citation. The provost made an excellent address about the close friendship between Jones and the residents of St. Andrews. Jones then moved to the lectern. He decided to forget about the notes he had in his jacket pocket. He said among other things, "You people have a sensitivity and an ability to extend cordiality in an ingenious way." He spoke of the Old Course: "The more you study it, the more you love it, and the more you love it, the more you study it." Near the end of his talk, he said, "I could take out of my life everything except my experiences at St. Andrews, and I would still have a rich and full life." It is on such occasions that one feels that there is a singular communication among people involved in golf. No other sport provides anything like it.

The Women's World Amateur Team Championship got underway six years after the men's. Twenty-five countries sent teams of three players to France in October 1964, where the competition was held at the charming St. Germain Golf Club some 20 miles from Paris. In a tight and exciting, 72-hole match, the home team prevailed by a single stroke when Catherine Lacoste finished with a dramatic 73 near the end of the final day. The 19-year-old daughter of René Lacoste, the tennis champion, and Thion de la Chaume, who had won the British Ladies' championship in 1927 at Newcastle County Down in Ireland, Catherine went on to win the 1967 United States Women's Open on the wonderful course that Twomey and Flynn designed for the Cascades Golf Club in Hot Springs, Virginia. Two years later she added the British Ladies,' which was played at Portrush in northern Ireland. She then went on to wrap up the bundle by winning the United States Women's Amateur at the Los Colinas Country Club in Irving, Texas, where the temperature that week fre-

10 The Legendary Tree, *Winged Foot, Mamaroneck, New York*

quently climbed above one hundred degrees. The following year, 1970, Catherine Lacoste was married and retired from tournament golf.

Shell Oil, that huge international consortium which keeps its ear to the ground, demonstrated its awareness of the golf boom by bringing out in the early 1960s "Shell's Wonderful World of Golf," an hour-long show, in techni-color, which became a popular Sunday-afternoon diversion in the United States and ran for almost a decade. Each week a leading American pro played an 18-hole match, at medal play, against a leading foreign pro — say, Roberto De Vicenzo of Argentina or Dai Rees of Wales. Shell had entrée to the best and most private golf clubs in the world, such as the Royal and Ancient, Pine Valley in western New Jersey, and Royal Melbourne in Australia. The show's hosts were Gene Sarazen and Jimmy Demaret, and the series exuded the genuine spirit of the game. Golf fans around the globe can still purchase tapes of the most popular matches for their VCRs.

In the decades following the Second World War, the best amateurs in the United States, with few exceptions, sooner or later turned professional. Seeking a touch of distinction, an increasing number of colleges in this country, most of them in the South and Southwest, began to build outstanding golf teams by awarding golf scholarships to promising players. Sooner or later most of these young men turned professional. Arnold Palmer, who had attended Wake Forest, joined the PGA Tour shortly after winning the U.S. Amateur in 1954, for the tournament prize money on the professional circuit was steadily rising. At the same time, interest in the Walker Cup matches was never higher on both sides of the ocean than it was during the 25 years following the war. The top amateurs relished the special atmosphere and spirit that characterized the series on both sides of the ocean. So did the galleries. In the end it all came down to the high personal qualities of the individual players who were at the heart of the competition for many years — fellows like Harvie Ward, Billy Joe Patton, Charlie Coe, Bill Campbell, Bud Taylor, Bill Hyndman, and Ed Updegraff of the United States, and Gerald Micklem, Joe Carr, Reid Jack, Michael Lunt, Michael Bonallack, R.D.B.M. (Right Down the Bloody Middle) Shade, and Rodney Foster of Britain and Ireland. Throughout the postwar period, the British did not win a Walker Cup match until 1971. That spring, at St. Andrews, they seemed hopelessly outmatched: they had won only a half-point in the four foursomes in the morning of the second and final day. In the afternoon, however, they rallied, took six of the eight singles, and, for the first time since 1938, carried off the Walker Cup, 13-11. Michael Bonallack, making his eighth appearance in the series, captained the winning team. Bonallack's record also includes five victories in the British Amateur. For some time now, he has been the secretary of the R and A, and, characteristically, he has made that complex administrative post look like a piece of cake. . . . Oh yes. One other thing. Sooner or later everything comes to pass. In 1989, at the Peachtree Golf Club outside Atlanta, the British and Irish team won the Walker Cup on American soil for the first time, and the young man who scored the decisive point had developed his game while attending Wake Forest on an Arnold Palmer golf scholarship.

Three years after he had turned professional, Arnold Palmer arrived at the top by winning the 1958 Masters with some daring shotmaking under pressure. (He reminded the old-timers of Hagen.) He won the Masters a second time in 1960 by holing a slippery five-foot sidehill putt on the seventy-second green. He went

11. Rough by the Sea, *Turnberry, Scotland*

12. The 8th at Merion, *Ardmore, Pennsylvania*

on to capture the 1960 U.S. Open at Cherry Hills, outside Denver, with a closing 65. (He birdied six of the first seven holes.) Late that summer Palmer made his first trip to Europe. At Portmarnock, near Dublin, he teamed with Snead to win the Canada Cup. He continued on to St. Andrews, which was the obvious club to host the British Open that summer when the championship celebrated its hundredth anniversary. Considering that this was the first time that Palmer had encountered the cold rain off the sea, the thrashing winds, and the subtle and slippery greens that only a local caddie can read, he adjusted exceedingly well and finished second, a stroke behind the winner, Kel Nagle of Australia. The following summer when the Open was played at Birkdale in Lancashire, close by the Irish Sea, Palmer won it, edging out Dai Rees by a stroke. He was on the edge of disaster a number of times. For instance, on the fifteenth hole in the third round, he was able to slash a wedge recovery from a wicked lie in willow scrub almost onto the green, and on his final round he somehow managed to gouge his ball out of a patch of creeping blackberry bushes with his six-iron and muscle it onto the green. Things were quite different when Palmer returned to Scotland the next summer to defend his title at Troon. A severe draught had ruined the greens and the fairways, and the course became a test of a golfer's skill at pinpointing his tee shots and then judging where on the fairway to land each approach shot so that the ball would take the bounce he was counting on and end up on the green in the vicinity of the pin. After 36 holes, Palmer led by two strokes. On the last two rounds he continued to drive the ball almost perfectly and to improvise a succession of the delicate touch shots. He made a few putts and ended up winning by six strokes.

Arnold Palmer revitalized the British Open singlehandedly. In 1963 or thereabouts, ambitious golfers from the green corners of the world have made it a point to fly to Scotland or England each summer and try to qualify for a place in the British Open's starting field, if they haven't already earned one. Most of the game's best players have managed to produce some of their best shotmaking in the British Open. Gary Player, the astonishing athlete from South Africa, broke

through in the British at 22 in 1959 with rounds of 70 and 68 on the last day at Muirfield. He went on to win the championship at Carnoustie in 1968 and at Lytham in 1974. (Player, by the way, is one of the four golfers who have won all four major championships. The others are Sarazen, Hogan, and Nicklaus.) Nicklaus was 26 when he won the British for the first time, at Muirfield in 1966. He had already captured the other three majors: the U.S. Open in 1962, at Oakmont, after a playoff with Palmer; the Masters in 1963; and our PGA Championship in 1963 at the Dallas Country Club. Many of our accomplished professionals have won at least one British Open. Lee Trevino, for instance, carried it off in 1971 and 1972. Tom Watson, as we all know, has won it five times, in 1975, 1977, 1980, 1982, and 1983. In 1977 at Turnberry, Watson and Nicklaus, tied for the lead after 36 holes, were paired on the last day when the last two rounds were played in cold and blustery weather. Nicklaus had a pair of 66s. Watson, after a 66 in the morning, brought in a 65 in the afternoon, thanks to an amazing stretch drive: two pars and four birdies on the last six holes.

We must not fail to mention some of the unforgettable achievements that have taken place here at home during the last 30 or so years. Mary Kathryn "Mickey" Wright, a handsome and bright young lady from the San Diego area, joined the LPGA Tour in 1955 and quickly began to attract attention. Tall, strong, and highly motivated, she could hit the ball a long way and with rare precision. In the summer of 1961, she reached her peak in winning her third U.S. Women's Open on the long and arduous Lower Course of the Baltusrol Golf Club in Springfield, New Jersey, where she put together rounds of 72, 80, 69, and 72 and won by six shots. It wasn't her scoring that one remembers — she putted poorly on her second round — but the power, accuracy, and flight of her tee shots and her approaches with her long and middle irons. On the morning round on the final day, Mickey was around in 69 with six birdies. In the afternoon, she put her approach shots no farther than 20 feet from the flagstick on hole after hole but took two putts on every green. I have never seen another woman play that kind of golf or anything close to it. Mickey won the U.S. Women's Open in 1958, 1959, 1961, and 1964, her last full season on the tour. In her spare time between rounds and tournaments, she read exhaustively, studied French, practiced the guitar, went fishing, and listened to her library of classical recordings on her portable record player. When she had had her fill of the nomadic life, Mickey settled in Dallas. She has had no trouble keeping busy.

Where does one start when he wants to say a few words about Jack Nicklaus? The 1965 Masters might be a good place. The golfer who can regularly carry the ball close to 250 yards off the tee has a decided advantage at the Augusta National, for his drives will frequently land on the long downslopes of the hills and pick up many additional yards. In the 1965 Masters, for example, Nicklaus led off with a 67, added an acceptable 71, took full advantage of the ideal conditions on the third day and posted a 64, and finished with a nice 69 for a record-breaking total of 271. This prompted Bob Jones to remark at the presentation ceremonies, "Jack is playing an entirely different game — a game I'm not even familiar with." It is not sufficiently appreciated, but Nicklaus, for all of his confidence and competitive toughness, is one of the game's authentic sportsmen. Let me give you an example. On the afternoon of the final day of the 1969 Ryder Cup match at Birkdale, Nicklaus, who had been playing mediocre golf, met Tony Jacklin, the rising young English star, in the last singles. As it turned out, the outcome of the team match depended on the outcome of the Nicklaus-Jacklin match. All even coming to the eighteenth, a strong par four, both men left their approach shots a good distance from the pin on that dangerous green. Neither of their approach putts left them with simple tap-ins. Nicklaus was faced with a hard-to-read four-footer for his par. He worked on it for several minutes and made it. Jacklin now had to hole a tricky two-and-a half-footer to halve not only his singles but the team match. He was just beginning to work on his putt when Nicklaus walked over, conceded it, and stuck out his hand. The final score was U.S. 16, G.B. 16, and the cup remained in the United States' possession. Most of Nicklaus's teammates, eager to feel that they had successfully beat-

en back the challenge of the British and Irish team, did not appreciate Jack's sporting gesture and let him know it. By the way, Jack's record number of major victories presently stands at 20: two U.S. Amateurs, three British Opens, four U.S. Opens, five PGA Championships, and six masters, the last in 1986 at the age of 46. He didn't look too bad either when he edged out Chi Chi Rodriguez at Oakland Hills in their playoff for the 1991 U.S. Seniors championship.

There are a few more topics to be addressed, briefly. To begin with, as we are all happily aware, in the last dozen or so years the golfers of Great Britain and Ireland have at length regained their old prominence. Two men have been principally responsible for this. The first is Tony Jacklin. The bright and spirited son of a truck driver, Jacklin drifted into golf at an early age. Bent on improving his game, he came to this country and spent a couple of winters on the PGA Tour. In 1969, he broke through in the British Open, the first native son to do this since Max Faulkner in 1951. The following year, Jacklin came over for the U.S. Open. At the recently completed Hazeltine National, near Minneapolis — the course was in bad shape after a hard winter — he was one of the few players who was able to cope with the crusty fairways, inconsistent greens, and the constantly changing wind. He moved out in front on the opening round with a 71 and consolidated his lead with a pair of 70s. When he opened his clubhouse locker on the morning of the fourth and final day, he found that a one-word note had been placed inside it: *Tempo.* Two of his friends, Tom Weiskopf and Bert Yancey, had put it there. Jacklin went out and finished with another well-managed 70. His margin of victory was seven strokes. I mention this anecdote because it may help to underline Jacklin's exceptional personal appeal, which, in combination with his unblinking practicality, helps to explain the success he enjoyed when he was asked in 1983 to captain the European Ryder Cup team, an aggregation of Scottish, English, Welsh, Irish, German, and Spanish golfers. (This change in the format had been established in 1979.) In Jacklin's first year, the European team was defeated 14 1/2 - 13 1/2 at the PGA National Golf Club in Palm Beach

Gardens, Florida, but it gained possession of the cup in 1985 at the Belfry Golf Club in Sutton Coldfield, England, 16 1/2 - 11 1/2. (Great Britain had last won the cup back in 1957.) In 1987, the European team held off a fired-up American team with a brave rally down the stretch at Muirfield Village Golf Club, in Dublin, Ohio. Back at the Belfry in 1989, the Europeans escaped with a tie (and held onto the cup) when several American players lost their poise on the finishing holes. Jacklin, feeling that he had accomplished what he had been asked to do, decided that it was time for him to step down.

The second man who helped to restore British golf to its former eminence was Severiano (Seve) Ballesteros. The son of a Spanish fisherman, he had learned the game on the excellent course that had been built for the wealthy families who lived in the nearby city of Santander on the Bay of Biscay. Seve turned professional at the age of

13. The Country Club, *Brookline, Massachussetts, scene of three U.S. Opens, including the shocking Ouimet victory over Britain's Harry Vardon and Ted Ray in 1913*

17 and went to England to seek his fortune. He could hit the ball huge distances but had trouble controlling it under tournament pressure. In 1979, when he was 22, he managed to stay in contention at Lytham on the last day of the British Open with a series of unbelievable recovery shots. He then collected himself, holed some big putts, and went on to win the championship by five strokes. An enthralling player to watch — nothing pleased him as much as conceiving and somehow bringing off impossible recovery shots — Ballesteros proceeded to carry off a high percentage of the big-money tournaments in Europe and around the globe, but, more significantly, he led the field in the Masters in 1980 and 1983, and went on to win his second British Open at St. Andrews in 1984 and his third back at Lytham in 1988. The admiration and respect that Ballesteros and Jacklin have for each other was the basis of the surprising success the European Ryder Cup team has enjoyed.

When graying golfers look back at the U.S. Open, the game's most important championship for decades now, an almost endless succession of memories is still clearly in focus. For example, Billy Casper, completely at ease in 1959 on the West Course at the Winged Foot Golf Club in Westchester County, New York, is in the process of using only 114 putts over the 72 holes of the championship; Julius Boros, another player known for his low-key approach to a nerve-racking game, is as relaxed as ever in outplaying Arnold Palmer and Jackie Cupit in their playoff for the 1963 Open at The Country Club, in Brookline: he brought in a 70, the lowest round of the championship; Ken Venturi, after wobbling badly in the intense heat in the 1965 Open at Congressional, outside Washington, D.C., is making his way down the seventy-second fairway, both exhausted and elated; Lee Trevino, at Oak Hill in Rochester in 1968, is putting together rounds of 69, 68, 69, and 69 to become the first golfer to break 70 on all four rounds of our Open; Johnny Miller, six shots off the pace at the start of the fourth round at Oakmont in 1973, jumps off with four consecutive birdies on the rain-soaked course, picks up three more birds on the back nine, posts a 63, a record low round for the championship, and wins the Open by a stroke; Jack Nicklaus is nailing down the championship in 1972, the first time it was held at Pebble Beach, south of San Francisco, when, on the last round, he rips a two-iron through a strong head wind on the dangerous par-three seventeenth and barely misses a hole in one when the ball, after landing inches short of the cup, hops up, hits the flagstick, and then spins itself out three inches away; Tom Watson, in 1982, when the Open returned to Pebble Beach, overtakes Nicklaus late in the final round when, after pulling his two-iron into the thick rough some 20 feet to the left of the flagstick on the seventeenth, he opens the face of his sand wedge, cuts across the ball, drops it softly on the edge of the green, and watches the ball break slowly for the pin, hit the middle of it, and tumble into the cup. Last but not least, Raymond Floyd, not the prettiest golfer in the world but one of the best under pressure, at long last wins the Open in 1986 at Shinnecock Hills on Long Island. P. J. Boatwright, had set the course up perfectly, and Floyd, rising to the occasion, caught and passed the leaders with some bold shotmaking on the last seven holes.

A final reflection: In the fast-paced modern world in which the telephone, automobile, television set, pharmacy, and liquor store play all too prominent roles, golf can be an invaluable boon. When you hurry to the golf course after dinner to get in nine holes or as many as you can before dark, the hush of twilight slows you down. The long shadows of the tall trees in the rough bring out the rises and falls in the fairways and the subtle breaks in the green you are now walking onto. The green looks and feels almost like velvet, and this amuses you because it's so corny. You find you have a much slower putting stroke and a keener touch than you do in the morning or afternoon. You hit your next drive well, and so do the old friends you are playing with. At that hour you really hear the sound of your tee shot. As goes without saying, you are more aware of sounds than you are at any other part of the day, even early morning. You hear dogs barking in the distance and someone putting his car into the garage. You hit a pretty good iron — it probably finished just short of the green — and watch the western sky changing to darker shades of orange and gold. The wind stirs in the bushes and trees. The friends you are playing with are as aware of the spell of evening as you are. There is no need to talk. As the twilight deepens and the sky changes to gold and purple and a thin streak of crimson, you are absolutely pleased with life, and your friends feel the same way. You are not surprised by this. All of you have spent some of the happiest hours of your lives, from early boyhood, on that pleasant stretch of fairways and woods and small streams. You all putt out and, without exchanging a word, head for the clubhouse. These moments on the golf course at sundown are the only times when you feel totally in touch with the world, not just today's world but the world that has been whirling for centuries. As all golfers know, moments like these are just one of the ways in which golf enriches your life.

— Herbert Warren Wind

18

The
SPIRIT OF GOLF

14. Checking In at Nairn, *The Old Clubhouse, Scotland*

20

The everlasting debate to decide who is or was the greatest golfer of the modern era can never be really conclusive. Methods and materials improve in much the same way as memories grow ever shorter. The fascinating thing is that there is never a let-up in the enthusiasm for such indeterminate arguments.

I like the idea of picking a team on Ryder or Walker Cup lines, which I am more than confident could hold its own against any other team representing the Rest of the World in a two-day match of 18-hole foursomes and singles.

My modern era would embrace the last 50 years, which would neatly and conveniently exclude the first great triumvirate of Vardon, Braid, and Taylor, who could fairly be said to have been on the wane after the First World War. Although all three played in the first professional team match against the Americans at Gleneagles in 1921, they were not included in the British side which was given such a drubbing in the first Ryder Cup match six years later.

With most British Ryder Cup and Walker Cup teams, whatever the method of qualification and selection decided upon — and this changes after practically every match — half the team virtually chooses itself. And so it is with my 12 greatest players to oppose the Rest.

For example, from the generation in its prime in the first decade of the last half-century, Bobby Jones, Walter Hagen, and Gene Sarazen can hardly be opposed, even though no British players get a look in. George Duncan, Arthur Havers, Ted Ray, and Tommy Armour would all merit consideration but would end up playing for the Rest of the World.

From the '30s and '40s, Henry Cotton and Byron Nelson are the obvious names with which to conjure. Ben Hogan stands alone and unchallenged in the '50s, although Bobby Locke is not far behind him and is perhaps the most underrated member of the team.

I fully appreciated the timeless authority of Locke's eccentric method, unnerving as it was to stand on the next fairway to Locke's right and find myself the exact point of aim for one of the maestro's 100-yard pitch shots! Locke's banana shaped, hooked trajectory grew ever more pronounced as he struggled to maintain his length. But such a bizarre method would have fallen to pieces were it not founded on the most flawless natural rhythm — possibly of all time.

Since Locke is unquestionably one of the six best putters in the history of the game, there is no doubt of the validity of his selection. Not even his defective eyesight — damaged when his car was destroyed on a level crossing some years ago — blunted his uncanny touch around the greens.

Although I used to doubt the wisdom of old campaigners such as Locke, Dai Rees, and Max Faulkner continuing in tournament play when well past their prime — like prize-fighters slipping inevitably into oblivion — each had so much still to offer to the youthful student apart from their unquenchable competitive urge.

While on the subject of Rees, I feel he would make an ideal captain for the Rest of the World side as possibly the best match-play golfer of his lifetime, with due respect to Eric Brown, whose Ryder Cup singles record was second to none.

With five British Open titles and countless other victories behind him, Peter Thomson is an obvious contender for one of the places lower in the order of my world dozen. But despite the mental strength that made him one of the most formidable thinkers in the professional ranks — one of golf's few intellectuals — he had a glaring weakness. Thomson's undistinguished record in America and his petulant attitude to golf in that country stands out all the more because it comes from such an intelligent man.

Jack Nicklaus shares Thomson's dislike of huge greens and excessive watering so prevalent in America, but the difference between the two is that Jack has proved his greatness by mastering all sorts and conditions of golf courses. Nicklaus walks into my team, as

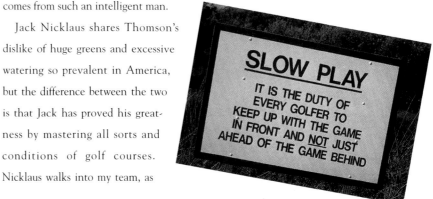

SLOW PLAY
IT IS THE DUTY OF EVERY GOLFER TO KEEP UP WITH THE GAME IN FRONT AND <u>NOT</u> JUST AHEAD OF THE GAME BEHIND

do Arnold Palmer, Gary Player, and Lee Trevino, all four outstanding in a decade when to be so was never more difficult. But Thomson is relegated to the Rest.

Completing my 12 is the name of Sam Snead, whose method and rhythm have stood the test of time every bit as well as that of Locke. Snead's poetic natural grace is as orthodox as the outlandish method of the portly South African is astonishing. But Snead has never been in the same league as Locke as a putter, a fact that would influence me to play him and Cotton low in the order, possibly as foursome partners. Apart from Thomson, the pair with most pressing claims who figured unsuccessfully in my short list were Billy Casper and Roberto de Vicenzo. In a nutshell, Casper's record abroad was as poor as Thomson's was in America. And while de Vicenzo's method was as indestructible as that of Snead or Locke, the Argentinian grandfather lacked the essential hardness to succeed in match play.

My window is open for wagers.

15. Oyster Reef, *Hilton Head Island, South Carolina*

On arriving for my first visit to Lahinch Golf Club in County Clare, at the very edge of the Atlantic Ocean, with the commanding backdrop of the majestic Cliffs of Moher just across the bay to the north, I was mystified by an empty wooden barometer case hanging in the porch containing only a small postcard on which was written the terse message "SEE GOATS."

It was a rarely beautiful, cloudless and warm morning with little wind. My foursome could hardly wait to present ourselves to the club's genial secretary to get permission to play one of the greatest courses in Ireland and, for that matter, the entire world.

The secretary could not have made us more welcome, so I finally felt justified in asking him about that card pinned to the inside of the barometer, whose message had completely bewildered me.

"Well, sir, it's like this, you see," he replied in splendid singsong Irish brogue. "We have a herd of goats that roams the golf course, and they are great judges of our very variable local weather. When those strange devils are out grazing around the golf course, the members know that if they can't see them the goats are far enough afield to indicate that the weather will be fit to play for the foreseeable future. But even on the best of days if they see the goats heading back to the clubhouse or even huddled in the porch, we know that the bad weather is on its way, and our members will need their umbrellas and waterproof clothing if they care to venture out. Better still, the older and wiser brethren know that they would be better off in the bar."

In the early '70s, big, strong, and talented Scottish professional David Huish surprised a fine international field in the John Player Classic at Turnberry, but not himself, by establishing a clear lead after two rounds of the now defunct, once very lucrative tournament.

Huish, a family man, was sufficiently devoted to his job as club professional at the historic West Links, North Berwick Golf Club near Edinburgh, that he limited his tournament appearances to an occasional foray.

When I interviewed Huish that evening, I suggested that if he managed to hang on and win the event, surely he would have to consider playing the British tournament circuit on a regular basis.

Huish's reaction was one of horror that I should even pose such a stupid question. His eyebrows shot up and he replied emphatically in his broad Scottish accent, "Heavens, no; no bloody fear! Why would I ever do such a daft thing as that when I can stand in my shop every day of the year and watch out of the window as a thankfully never-ending stream of caramel chewers thrash their Dunlop 65s (golf balls) joyously into the bay? That, my man, is what I call job security."

Huish duly faded out of contention, and the following Monday morning was looking out of that window, and smiling with satisfaction, knowing that he would be sleeping in his own bed that evening.

The perennial pro-am player is in many ways a strange animal, and definitely not an endangered species. It has always amazed me how many stiff and staid captains of industry are prepared, even eager, to make fools of themselves in public on the golf course, a situation they would never allow to occur anywhere else. Men of dignity and business acumen when sailing through the corridors of power with a flock of underlings in their wake become semiparalytic when overcome by first-tee nerves. Yet they will fall over each other in a furious dogfight behind the scenes to ensure a featured pairing alongside Jack Nicklaus rather than some unknown rookie, although they are fully aware of the almost certain consequences. Five thousand people will be clustered around the first tee to watch Nicklaus crunch the ball, while the rookie will probably start in total obscurity from the tenth tee in the company of his current girlfriend and a couple of close friends. Of course, any chance of our hero hitting even a halfway decent first drive evaporates under Nicklaus's baleful glare, while those 5,000 spectators, many of them average golfers themselves, will chuckle and rub their hands with gleeful sadism as our man dribbles his ball along the ground, just reaching the ladies' tee. Naturally he could have taken the pressure off himself and played an enjoyable, uncluttered game alongside the rookie in question.

But as a perennially masochistic pro-am player myself for these past 30-odd years, I know only too well that, deep down in my heart, for reasons that defy logic, playing in pleasant obscurity is not what I crave. If I am going to suffer a round that will take the best part of six hours to complete, I want to rub shoulders with the best and later show off the mandatory photograph of our illustrious group, duly mounted, to my children and grandchildren. I'll probably tell them how well I played, for good measure!

There is no guarantee, however, that a pro-am will be a pleasant experience, even if you happen to play the best golf of your life. There are a few, thankfully very few, professional golfers who have gained well-deserved notoriety for their scornful disdain of their amateur partners, on whom their very living really depends. This shortsighted bunch is very much outnumbered by those who are only too aware of the value of pro-ams as a powerful public relations exercise.

I can share a personal story of such an experience. Although I have since become a friend, admirer, and commentating colleague of Tom Weiskopf, I should point out that this most magnificently elegant of world-class players did not earn his nickname "Terrible Tom" for nothing.

In early 1968 I was the pro-am guest of the long-defunct National Airlines at its tournament at the Country Club of Miami to inaugurate the airline's service between that city, its home base, and London. I arrived several days in advance and worked diligently on my game, then played to a respectable five handicap. Poor Tom came down from the snows of Ohio, having just completed a compulsory period of army reserve training. His game was very short of its awesome best. And for eight glorious holes I outplayed him into the greens, constantly hitting my second shot or tee shots much closer to the hole. Imagine my chagrin when, on the eighth green, with my ball five feet from the hole and on Tom's line — but his ball was 20 feet farther away — he hissed, "Putt your _____ ball, and get out of the _____ way." I promptly three-putted, quickly fell apart, and did not speak to Weiskopf for five futile years, having written about the incident in the *Financial Times* and *Golf World* magazine (UK).

To Tom's eternal credit, he apologized by inviting me to his intimate dinner party at the Marine Hotel, Troon, to celebrate his Open Championship victory of 1973 — a memorable evening indeed — and we have laughed about the incident several times since.

There are two more types of perennial pro-am player who continually amaze me. The first jealously guards a low handicap, although his first swing tells his professional partner he has no earthly chance of playing to it, or even anywhere near it. As one

16. The Goats of Lahinch, *Ireland. If they're near the clubhouse, rain is sure; if they're on the course, play away!*

world-class professional golfer told me recently, "Before the end of the round, as his game becomes more and more unglued, this type of player will always look you squarely in the eye and say, 'I can honestly tell you this is the worst round I've played in 10 years,' or something to that effect. Can you imagine how many times he has to tell that story, and how many times I've heard it before?"

The vanity of this type of amateur golfer is obviously monumental. But I infinitely prefer his sadly deluded type to the chap, or in American parlance "sandbagger," who checks in with a 16 handicap and from his very first practice swing shows his professional that he is unlikely to drop more than half a dozen strokes to par. He rarely, if ever, does. Of course, there are high-handicap golfers who enjoy magical days in the sun, and these are very often professionals at another sport who are not mortally afraid and totally unhinged by playing in front of sizable crowds, and who possess obvious ability at all ball games — natural athletes. To me there is nothing more enjoyable than being in the company of a true amateur who

> Walter Hagen, the PGA champion four times running from 1924, got a financial offer he couldn't refuse for an exhibition, which conflicted with a fifth attempt. Leo Diegel became the new PGA champion, but no one could find the trophy. Hagen had squirreled it away at his club manufacturers, and they discovered it!

is playing way over his head and is basking in the consequent euphoric glow. Goodness knows, such euphoria is destined to be very short-lived.

My own pro-am experiences have embraced farce, tragedy, comedy, and, on very few occasions, the ecstasy of victory.

My first "major" pro-am appearance was in the old, long-forgotten Bowmaker tournament at Sunningdale, England, in the company of the late, great Bobby Locke. I arrived hours ahead of my starting time, ever the neurotic, asked the caddie master for assistance, and was told my caddie was known as "One Tooth Jock." A giant, malodorous Scotsman in a too-long military greatcoat, cloth cap and laced-up boots emerged from the caddie shed, the solitary fang in his upper jaw hanging over his lower lip. We made for the practice tee, where I flailed away for what seemed like an age with no comment, just an inscrutable stare from my companion. And then I made my fatal mistake.

"Do you need lunch before we go at 12:52?" I asked Jock. "Yessir," he answered with his first display of transparent enthusiasm. I handed him a five-pound note, took my putter and four golf balls, and told him to meet me on the first tee at 12:45 by the clubhouse clock.

Needless to say, despite several appeals over the public address system, Jock failed to appear. My confusion was complete. Eventually the legendary Arthur Lees, Sunningdale's professional at the time, sent out a brand-new set of clubs and accessories and, totally embarrassed, we set out. We were walking up the hill from the seventh tee when I first heard the raucous strains of "Glasgow Belongs to Me," a famous Scottish ditty, and Jock heaved over the horizon towards us, stumbling dangerously, my bag of clubs slung across his chest.

"Where the hell have you been?" I asked him.

"Well, sir," he grinned frighteningly through a haze of Scotch whiskey fumes. "I set off with this group, sir. And after we had gone seven holes and nobody had asked me for a club, I realized I was with the wrong foursome, and came looking for you."

The best pro-am partner I ever had, bar none, was Gary Player. In the 1974

17. From the Rough, *Lahinch, Ireland*

La Manga Campo de Golf resort's pro-am played over 72 holes, the then owner of that splendid southern Spanish facility, American entrepreneur Greg Peters, conceived the idea that the professionals should not record their individual scores but rather take forward that of their team's best ball. It was a praiseworthy attempt to foster camaraderie between professionals and amateurs, and with the exuberant South African it worked like a charm. Each team played with a different professional every day, and we drew Player for the vital third round in 1974 or, as Gary calls it, "moving day." So determined was Player to make the three of us play to the summit of our capabilities, he mostly ran from amateur to amateur to coach us on every shot. I don't remember what phenomenally low total we posted as a team that marvelous day — I think it was 19-under par 53 — but it helped us to spreadeagle the field, and we won the event going away by seven shots with a record aggregate. And Player was the professional winner, hardly surprisingly.

The euphoria I experienced that magical day alongside the great Gary Player is unlikely to be repeated. But I keep on trying, and hoping. And I suppose that is what pro-ams are all about. They bring out the Walter Mitty in all of us hackers.

18. Ladies of the Club, *Edgartown, Massachusetts*

The slogan emblazoned on the cover of the 1992 Ladies Professional Golf Association's tour guide reads, "The Tour of the '90s." That may be, but what we are really witnessing is the greatest upsurge in the popularity of golf amongst ALL women in the history of the game.

David Foster, the Englishman who, as chairman and CEO of the vast Colgate-Palmolive empire, saw women's professional golf as a magnificent worldwide marketing vehicle for his company's products in the 1960s and 1970s, and promoted women's tournaments in all sectors of the globe, was perhaps a little ahead of his time. He was succeeded as chairman by a gentleman whose passion in the sporting field was yachting, and women's professional golf was dealt a body blow so severe it took years to recover.

But as Jack Frazee, chairman and CEO of Centel Corporation, who in 1992 at the Centel Classic put on a tournament offering the largest purse in the history of women's golf — $1.2 million, with a first prize of $180,000 — told me during the event, "How am I going to go home in this day and age and tell my mother, my wife, my daughters, or even the female shareholders in Centel Corporation that the prize money in women's golf should be inferior to that offered on the men's tour? Equal pay for equal work must be the pattern of the future in golf's fastest-growing area."

Women's golf has really seen three distinct generations or eras since its humble and uneasy beginnings in the professional arena in the late 1940s and 1950s, when such pioneers as Babe Zaharias, Peggy Kirk (now Kirk Bell), Patty Berg, Louise Suggs, Marilynn Smith and Betsy Rawls blazed a trail in comparative obscurity, largely for what is now regarded as small change, most often on scruffy public courses.

The legendary Mickey Wright did much to strengthen the hold of that first generation on the public's imagination by winning 45 tournaments between 1961 and 1964, four of them consecutively. The final round of the U.S. Women's Open was televised in 1963 for the first time, and Sears, Roebuck became the sport's first commercial sponsor for a three-year period.

But despite passing these memorable milestones, the LPGA Tour fell on hard times financially in the early 1970s until Ray Volpe was hired in 1975 as the association's first commissioner. As former vice-president of marketing for the National Hockey League, he brought all the right credentials to his new post. During his tenure as commissioner, prize money on the tour increased from $1.5 million to $6.4 million, with the average tournament purse increasing from $50,000 to $176,000. But perhaps Volpe's single most important contribution to the association's progress was made in the number of tour events televised — up from two annually to no fewer than 14, a fantastic achievement.

Volpe was helped enormously in enlarging the scope and popularity of women's golf and the tour by the emergence of the "second generation" of women golfers, a college-bred generation spearheaded by Nancy Lopez and Pat Bradley, while the incredible Kathy Whitworth soldiered valiantly on to an amazing record 88 tour victories between 1962 and 1985, the female equivalent in longevity and dominance of Sam Snead or Jack Nicklaus. But during the reign of the second generation, half a dozen players overshadowed their rivals to such an extent that to qualify for the Hall of Fame with as many as 30 victories seemed entirely feasible.

Things are vastly different today with the emergence of the "third generation" of women golfers, who almost entirely graduate to the tour via sophisticated college golf programs and are often athletes in other fields as well as being talented golfers. The tour has become fiercely competitive, with such great depth that as many as 50 players or more in any given week can win the tournament in progress. Multiple victories in a single season are, and will become, less frequent,

so it is obvious that the qualification regulations for the Hall of Fame have become more severe and demanding than those existing in any other sport. For instance, in 1991 there were 25 different winners of 37 events, and five players recorded first-time victories.

Since Charles S. Meachem, Jr., became commissioner of the LPGA in November 1990, he has done so much to enhance the image of women's golf that the sport is presently reaching new heights of popular appeal. As one might expect of a gentleman who had enjoyed previously a most successful 24-year career in broadcasting, Meachem has already achieved great success in that area. Significantly, the CBS television network carried two major women's professional tournaments in 1992 after an absence from the sport of nine years.

Meachem will certainly ensure that it becomes easier for a great golfer to achieve a place in the Hall of Fame, which currently contains only 12 players. Berg (57 career victories), Betty Jameson (10), Suggs (50), and Zaharias (31) were all inducted in 1951 to the previously named Women's Golf Hall of Fame established the previous year, and they were all similarly inducted into the current Hall of Fame established by the LPGA in 1967. The latter also includes Wright (1964 – 82 career victories), Whitworth (1975 – 88), Sandra Haynie (1977 – 42), Carol Mann (1977 – 38), JoAnne Carner (1982 – 42), Lopez (1987 – 44), and Bradley (1991 – 30). Those on the threshold of the Hall's portals as I write are Amy Alcott (stuck on 29 victories), Beth Daniel (27), Patty Sheehan (26), and Betsy King (25).

Meachem has set about honoring the great women golfers, the pioneers, on whom the LPGA and its members previously had largely turned a cruelly blind eye. When I was in Princeville, Kauai, in December 1991 for the JBP Cup World Women's Matchplay Championship, won by another rising young star Deb

Richard, Meachem honored the magnificent Hawaiian-born golfer Jackie Pung on her 70th birthday with a delightful dinner party, attended by many of the up-and-coming young golfers who were largely ignorant of Pung's past heroic exploits. Pung, a multiple winner on tour in the 1950s, was tragically disqualified from victory in the 1957 U.S. Open at Winged Foot for inadvertently signing an incorrect scorecard — a sort of female Roberto de Vicenzo. The fine members at Winged Foot had become so enamored of her personally and professionally that they raised enough money to give Pung more than the $1,800 won by the eventual winner Betsy Rawls.

The future of women's golf and the LPGA is surely as promising as its past has been mainly an uphill battle to achieve recognition in its own right, rather than the scorned poor relations of the men's and seniors' tours. The new breed comprises youngsters who are mostly as athletic as they are personable, and they are very aware of their duties as public relations representatives for their Association.

The 1949 British Open Championship played at Royal St. George's Golf Club in Sandwich, Kent, England, was won by Arthur D'Arcy (Bobby) Locke, a portly, 31-year-old South African who proved ruthless in demolishing a genial Irishman, Harry Bradshaw, by 12 strokes in the most one-sided 36-hole play-off in the history of this great event.

Locke, the son of a well-to-do men's outfitter from Germiston, nine miles outside Johannesburg, shot 67-68, to realize his life's ambition. Locke had started swinging a club at the age of four and had won the open and amateur championships of his native country by the time he was 17. He went on to capture the British Open on three subsequent occasions (1950, 1952, and 1957), during a decade in which he and Australian Peter Thomson completely dominated European golf.

The major difference between the two men, aside from their playing styles, was that whereas Thomson disliked most things American and never made a mark on the PGA Tour, Locke mounted the most successful one-man "invasion" of America in the modern era and possibly could have dominated American golf had he not been "banned" from playing on the American Tour by the PGA.

When Locke first arrived in the United States early in 1947 at the invitation of Sam Snead, a rivalry between him and Snead already existed. Locke, called "The Man from the Jungle," had humiliated Snead, then the British Open champion, the previous winter, in a series of exhibition matches throughout South Africa. Locke won 12 of 16 events, with two matches resulting in halves. His American rivals realized that such evidence proved that Locke was a player of substance, but the South African's physical appearance belied this fact.

Although he had flown 1,800 hours of missions during World War II, primarily as a bomber pilot in the Middle East, Locke came to America looking rather paunchy and broad in the beam. His tall, heavy build was accentuated by the florid, fleshy jowls and double chin that earned him another irreverent nickname, "Old Muffin Face." Locke's baggy, thick plus-fours, his formal, white, long-sleeved shirts and tightly knotted ties, which he wore even in the hottest, most humid weather, his soft white cap and white shoes made him look many years older and far less athletic than he actually was.

But it was primarily Locke's extraordinary swing and technique that caused the best American players to doubt his ability at first. The South African played with a pronouncedly bent left elbow in the style of his idol Walter Hagen and went far past the horizontal on the backswing. He aimed to the right of his target with every shot, made an exaggerated shoulder turn, and hit the ball with a looping hook. It was all singularly unimpressive, despite the ease and rhythm. Yet Locke almost invariably contrived to keep the ball in play. He was deadly

19. Playing through the Squall, *Dornoch, Scotland*

accurate around the greens and was by common consent the best putter the game had ever seen. Indeed, the cynics claimed that he was so ordinary a striker of the ball that he had to be a great putter to prevail.

Perhaps it was Locke's stately carriage and bearing on the golf course and his icy politeness both on and off it that infuriated his rivals. In the words of British golf columnist Pat Ward-Thomas, "The great burgo-magisterial curve of his figure, the unchanging rhythm of his movements, to me always suggested, and still do, the timelessness of the tide breaking upon a shore, over and over again, eternally, peaceful and inevitable."

20. A Typical Trap at Royal Liverpool (Holylake), *where the first British Amateur was held in 1885. In 1921 an informal match here between British and American amateurs inspired Mr. Herbert Walker, an American member of National Golf Links, to inaugurate the very next year what became the famous Walker Cup matches. John Ball, the only British golfer who ever won both the British Amateur (eight times!) and Open the same year, and Harold Hilton, who won the British Amateur four times and the U.S. Amateur in 1911 (at Apawamis), were both members of Royal Liverpool at the same time.*

Locke never forgot the bitter lesson he learned from Snead at the first postwar British Open at St. Andrews in 1946. He later wrote about it. With nine holes to play, Locke led Snead by one stroke. "I felt that I had my life's ambition within reach. I got excited. I started to walk fast and that geared me up. My concentration began to suffer. I made poor shots and lost. When I congratulated Sam, his reply was something I have never forgotten. He said quietly, 'Thanks, Bob, but it is just another tournament.' I decided that the sooner I acquired the same outlook, the better."

Never again was Locke's serene rhythm disturbed. Never again did he display the emotions that had made him a childhood club thrower. Locke became so completely self-disciplined that his only concession to his audience was to acknowledge their applause with a tip of his cap. His ponderous pace never again varied, despite strident complaints about his slow play. His remoteness and apparently smug self-assurance smacked of arrogance in the eyes of his rivals, and Locke encouraged their irritation, knowing full well that by doing so they would destroy themselves. "The Man From the Jungle" soon became more aptly named "The Archbishop."

Locke's impact on the American scene in 1947 could hardly have been more sensational. He won three of the first five events he entered, including the exclusive and prestigious Goodall Invitational at Charles River Country Club. During the Goodall, Locke was visibly furious with himself in the locker room after one round because he had been short of the hole with an approach putt. When asked why he was so made about such a minor slip, he answered, "It was an unforgivable blunder. I am never short on a putt, never."

This was probably interpreted as incredible conceit but, in fact, it was the premise on which Locke's game was based. While through the green he was generally content to play the percentages, he was never afraid to be aggressive with his old, faithful, rusty-bladed, hickory-shafted putter.

The hostility toward Locke among his American rivals possibly peaked soon after when George S. May, the Chicago entrepreneur, persuaded him to play in

21. Over the Wall, *North Berwick, Scotland. On the 13th hole, the course guide advises, "Don't argue with the wall, it's older than you."*

22. Western Gailes, *Scotland, 2nd hole*

his All-American extravaganza at Tam O'Shanter Country Club. Locke was paid appearance money of $5,000 and all expenses, and not surprisingly his home-bred combatants were furiously jealous. As though he enjoyed his notoriety, Locke led from the start, was tied by Ed "Porky" Oliver, then won a 36-hole play-off by six shots for a first-prize check of $7,000, at that time the biggest in the game.

Locke seemed invincible. Two weeks later, he won the Canadian Open at Scarboro Golf and Country Club in Toronto, and the following week he took the Columbus Invitational at Columbus CC by a whopping five strokes over Jimmy Demaret. Ben Hogan trailed Locke by 15 shots.

Despite missing 11 tournaments prior to The Masters and several more later in the season, Locke finished second on the 1947 money list to Demaret, winning $24,327 to the jovial Texan's $27,936. It had been a tour de force that the South African and no other foreigner since, including Locke's compatriot and protégé Gary Player, has ever equaled.

In 1949, within two months after his British Open win at Royal St. George's, Locke was banned for life by the PGA of America. His "crime" in the eyes of the committee was to have accepted invitations to play in an Inverness four-ball event in Toledo, Ohio, a few weeks after the British Open and subsequently in the Western Open — and not show up. At the time, the PGA of America had an agreement that required 30 days' notice be given before a player could withdraw from a tournament, unless he had a very good reason.

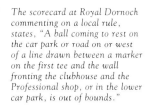

The scorecard at Royal Dornoch commenting on a local rule, states, "A ball coming to rest on the car park or road on or west of a line drawn between a marker on the first tee and the wall fronting the clubhouse and the Professional shop, or in the lower car park, is out of bounds."

Royal Liverpool Clubhouse

Locke believed that he had "good reason" for withdrawing after his victory at Royal St. George's. His sponsors, the manufacturers of the golf equipment he used, requested that he make himself immediately available for publicity work at their factories. Locke sent two cables explaining his reasons for pulling out of the American events, but, as he explained, "This aggravated the committee and the sponsors of the two tournaments. The upshot was that I was banned for life from all tournaments with which the PGA of America was connected. I was not even offered a hearing. I was summarily condemned and banished."

Less than a year after the ban was imposed, it was lifted, but it had had its effects on Locke, whose American forays thereafter became less and less frequent.

Instead of returning to America, Locke went to Britain, retained his Open title at Troon, and established a dominance in Europe that only Thomson could challenge.

But Locke was to enjoy one more very satisfying personal triumph in America. George S. May lured him over in August 1950 with a hugely lucrative guarantee to compete again in the All-American tournament at Tam O'Shanter and the World Championship of Golf that followed.

Locke came to the fourteenth hole at Tam O'Shanter needing four birdies to tie Lloyd Mangrum. The South African's trusty, rusty putter never served him better. He dispatched a 35-foot putt into the fourteenth hole for a birdie, a six-footer for another at the fifteenth, a 25-footer for a birdie at the sixteenth, and a 20-footer for the fourth birdie at the seventeenth. Locke played the eighteenth

conservatively for a par four and went into an 18-hole play-off the following day.

As he later wrote, "I was really out to win. Mangrum and I had little in common. I understand he had quite a bit of money bet on himself to beat me. Had he known how determined I was, I think he would have 'hedged' his bets. I holed a 15-foot putt on the second green for a birdie four, and taking a good look at Mangrum's face, decided that he was wounded. I then kept at him and never let up, and completed the round in 69 against his 73 to my complete satisfaction."

Pickings had now become richer and easier for Locke in Britain and on the Continent. In addition, his autographed line of golf clubs, produced by Slazenger, was selling well. So it was hardly surprising that Locke's appetite for the increasingly hard grind of the American Tour was never the same again. But not since the expatriate professionals from Britain, mainly the Scots, had brought the game to America had any foreigner struck such fear into the hearts and minds of the natives.

One of the greatest shots I ever witnessed was never recorded on television, for the very good reason that some of the Canadian Broadcasting Corporation's cables were joyously ablaze at the time. CBS was broadcasting the 1975 Canadian Open played over the fine Blue Course at Royal Montreal, and we took the CBC feed, which also had to be provided to their French- and English-speaking announcers — there was no love lost there — in separate booths. What consequently occurred was that the system was so overloaded and overheated it finally burst into flames around the French-speaking Canadian complex, watched with some glee by the English-speaking technicians who lifted not a finger to help. In fact, I asked a French-speaking Canadian technician later that day what he and his mates would have done had it been the English-speaking Canadian complex that had caught on fire.

"Monsieur, we would have taken an immediate lunch break and left the scene," he replied without so much as batting an eyelid.

Back to the miracle shot in question. The 426-yard sixteenth hole is one of four glorious finishing holes that tangle with a massive lake, in my opinion the best of the quartet. The drive is hit over the water, which also runs down the lefthand side of the fairway before crossing it in front of the green. There is just one island in that huge lake. Pat Fitzsimons was struggling to make the cut on the second day when he came to the tee, and hooked his ball, with half a gale blowing directly in his face, right on to the middle of it. The island has a diameter of about 10 yards.

Fitzsimons's caddy tested the waters and found them to be at least waist deep. At first he tried to carry Fitzsimons on his shoulders, but when he slipped Fitzsimons ventured off alone for his second shot, his four-iron held aloft like the rifle of an infantryman. He hit a fine shot to the green, all the way over water, made par, and thus inspired, he finished with two birdies for a 73 that could so easily have been 77 — incredible.

The bespectacled Fitzsimons's trademark when he was on the Tour was baggy cotton slacks, because he had an allergy to man-made fibers. As one wag commented as he emerged triumphantly from the water with them stuck sleekly to him, "Pat has never looked smarter in his life."

23. Sunningdale, *near London, England, 17th hole*

The golfers I have envied most during a 35-year-long love/hate relationship with the game have been those hundreds of thousands of amateurs to whom it is such a marvelous form of relaxation. After the rigors and pressures of their Monday-to-Friday existence, they don't expect miracles. They don't spend hours on the practice tee before going out in a vain search for a smooth new swing. They are quite happy with what they've got, even if in pure golfing terms that doesn't amount to a great deal. So they don't have a gleaming matched set in a leather bag as heavy and unwieldy as the average dustbin, but just a few rusty-shafted hand-me-downs in a Sunday bag that many generations of moths have been quite content to call home.

No, I haven't envied those hordes of contented hackers; I have loathed and despised them for their happy complacency. I always wanted so much more from golf than pure enjoyment — pure misguided fool.

As a youth the game came easily to me. For years I lived in ignorance of the most blissful kind about how difficult and humiliating golf can be. In the innocence of youth, I used to talk about the 20-foot putts I missed as if one should hole them all as a matter of course. For week upon week in the summer holidays, I would play 54 holes daily, analyzing each round in detail in the evenings. Imagination ran riot as I would quite contentedly plod round all alone, dreaming that if I could just finish with three pars the Open Championship would be mine.

As it turned out, I hardly ever won even a monthly medal. So where did it all go wrong? During two years away from playing the game on National Service, I played truant from my unit one day and just happened to see one of the great matches of all time. Tiny "Tiger" Poulton took the great Fred Daly to the thirtieth hole in their 18-hole encounter in the old *News of the World* match-play championship at Walton Heath. The diminutive Poulton looked every bit like a

This rather chauvinistic sign appears fronting the parking area at Royal Liverpool.

scruffy little terrier snapping at the heels of the big man from Belfast. I stood close by and watched in silent wonderment as the legendary Ulster man washed down a tongue sandwich with a glass of milk and went out, whistling incessantly, to thrash Peter Alliss, who had been waiting around for what must have seemed like an age, by 6 and 5.

On that fine day I became so obsessed by golf I determined to make it my life. The only trouble was that on my return to "civvy street" and the game, with a handicap of two, I had somehow discovered just how difficult golf is. The foolhardy bravery of youth had ebbed away to reveal a craven coward. I became happy to hole a three-foot putt, let alone talk of missing 20-footers. And instead of placing drives in the right area of the fairway with something approaching regularity, I hit, hoped, and sprayed the ball all over the place. But worst of all I developed one of the greatest abilities to shank short iron shots in the history of the game.

If there is a more insidious, self-destructive or soul-destroying shot in golf than the dreaded shank or socket, I have thankfully yet to experience it. The very words have a decidedly sharp ring to them.

For those unfamiliar with the term (is that possible?), shanking is hitting the ball off the angle of blade and shaft at a virtual right angle to the intended line of flight. Some say it is caused by "throwing" the club from the top outside the line, while others will tell you that it is caused by quickly rotating the wrists to take the clubhead too quickly inside the line. Perhaps the mystique about shanking has prevailed because not even the best teachers seem able to cure the worst sufferers.

I discovered just how infectious this shot can be when, on playing in my first-ever major pro-am at Wollaton Park, a lovely course on the outskirts of Nottingham, I hit two reasonably satisfactory shots just short of the first green into the teeth of a considerable cold breeze and driving rain. Five pitch shots

24. Gleneagles, The Queen's Course, Auchterarder, Scotland. Legend has it that the name Gleneagles emerged from that time in Scottish history when a French religious sect settled in a valley or glen in Scotland. The area they inhabited was then called "Glen Eglise" (Church Glen). But the natives couldn't pronounce it quite that way . . . so . . . "Gleneagles."

25. Mighty Cruden Bay, *near Aberdeen, Scotland*

later with my wedge, I had circled the green in an anticlockwise direction without ever getting closer to the putting surface.

My partner Neil Coles, mild and impeccably mannered as ever, "smiled through cold teeth," as the saying goes, and told me to pick up my ball and wait for him at the next tee. Alas, the second hole was a shortish par three, and after two tee shots had squirted away to the right over the out-of-bounds fence, I didn't need further directions. I scurried away in anguish to the third tee.

Thankfully my golf improved by leaps and stayed in bounds, and Coles was nothing short of sensational. We came to the last hole with him requiring a par for a 65 and victory. That knowledge duly unhinged me, and my second shot was shanked to the right and out of bounds in the twinkling of an eye. Coles followed suit. As he fixed me with a baleful glare, I finally realized how quickly and devastatingly the "disease" can spread. I leave with you a serious thought, however. Every time I shank so badly and often that I consider giving up the game for good, I recall the letter from a Peter Rose, of Newport, Gwent, which he concluded thus: "If one could guarantee not to shank, what would be the point of playing the bloody game?"

If one accepts the premise that Bobby Jones was the best amateur golfer of all time, and there are many who simply rate him the best golfer, amateur or professional, then who is or was the second-best amateur?

In the course of a rewarding and long-lasting correspondence I enjoyed with the prominent British amateur international Eustace Storey, a contemporary of Jones when both were at the height of their powers, Storey continually pressed Jones's claims to have been the best there ever was. "No one has ever been or ever will be as good as he (Jones) was," he wrote, and he cited two powerful examples of Jones's prowess.

Storey described how he and Cyril Tolley played the eventual winner, Harrison "Jimmie" Johnston, and Jones on the eve of the 1929 U.S. Amateur championship at Pebble Beach. The British pair were eminently satisfied to have got round in approximately 73 strokes apiece. The only trouble was that Jones had scored 65. The following year Storey recalled that Jones started 3-4-3-2-4 against Sid Roper, a coal miner from Bulwell Forest, in the first round of the Amateur at St. Andrews. Roper's five pars of 4-4-4-4-5 left him four down but he lost only by 3 and 2. Jones drove into the cottage bunker at the 427-yard fourth hole — not intended to punish tee shots. Jones then holed his second shot from the sand; he later called it the best shot he ever hit. It was in that year, 1930, that Jones pulled off the Grand Slam by winning the Open and Amateur championships of both Britain and America, a feat that will almost certainly never be equaled.

The *Golf Journal*, published bimonthly by the United States Golf Association, in 1981 came up with its findings on the second-best amateur, having canvassed the opinions of seven great players and Joe Dey, the executive director of the USGA for 35 years until 1969. More than one "judge" pointed out the folly of comparing golfers from different eras, and some doubted the wisdom of excluding brilliant players who had enjoyed brief but tremendously successful careers before turning professional.

Dey also cited the foolishness of ignoring the legendary Australian amateur Ivo Whitton, who once played off a handicap of plus eight and won the first of his five Australian Opens at the age of 18 in 1912 by five strokes from two Sydney professionals. After active service in the First World War as a lieutenant in the Royal Horse Artillery in Greece and Bulgaria, which deprived him of many championship opportunities when in his prime, Whitton won his final Australian Open in Sydney in 1931. He came from eight strokes back to pip Jim Ferrier, later to become U.S. PGA champion in 1947, and the left-handed Harry Williams by a single stroke. Whitton rated his 72 (out in 33) that day in a fierce gale the best round he ever played. Whitton also won the Australian amateur twice, in 1921 and 1922.

Of the judges, then USGA vice-president William C. (Bill) Campbell, Walker Cup players Charles (Chuck) Kocsis, Jess Sweetser, Willie Turnesa, and Charlie Yates, and Thomas E. Cheehan did not even mention a British player. All but one of the judges, however picked Francis Ouimet, who, as an unknown 20-year-old, beat British professionals Harry Vardon and Ted Ray in a play-off for the 1913 U.S. Open at The Country Club, Brookline. Ouimet had learned to play as a caddie at this club on the outskirts of Boston. He remained an amateur all his life, won the U.S. Amateur twice in 1914 and 1931, was a member of the first American Walker Cup team in 1922, and became the first American to become captain of the Royal and Ancient Golf Club of St. Andrews — Dey himself being the second, Campbell the third.

Dey nominated Royal Liverpool, Hoylake's duo of John Ball, who won the British amateur eight times between 1888 and 1912 and became the first amateur to win the Open at Prestwick in 1890, and Harold Hilton on his short list of six that also included Jack Nicklaus, Ouimet, Charles "Chick" Evans, and Jerome Travers. Apart from Bob Jones, Hilton was the only amateur twice to win the Open Championship or the U.S. Open as an amateur, winning the British title at Muirfield in 1892 and at Hoylake in 1897. Hilton was also the only Briton to win the U.S. Amateur — in 1911 — when he also won the British amateur title for the third of four times.

At least Dey gave an honorable mention to Michael Bonallack for win-

ning his five British amateur titles and Irishman Joe Carr his three. But neither had a record to speak of in many visits to the United States, where the big ball regularly betrayed them.

Evans, like Ouimet a caddie, also like Ouimet won the U.S. Amateur twice and U.S. Open once, and actually played in no fewer than 50 U.S. Amateurs — astonishing longevity.

He won both championships in the same year in 1916. The nonchalant Travers won the 1915 U.S. Open and promptly retired, having won the U.S. Amateur in 1907 and 1908, 1912, and 1913 previously.

In my own belief that golfers of different eras can hardly be fairly compared objectively, I present my short list of six for the title of the best amateur of the past 50 years — all of whom I have seen play — disqualifying all who have since turned professional.

The Walker Cup

How about this sextet? Charlie Coe, U.S. Amateur champion in 1949 and 1958 and runner-up in the 1951 British, who also lost to Nicklaus at the final hole of the 1959 U.S. Amateur final; William C. (Bill) Campbell, the U.S. champion in 1964 whose Walker Cup career spanned 24 years, and who was later the U.S. Senior amateur champion; Vinny Giles, who won the U.S. championship in 1972 and the British in 1975; Bonallack; Carr; and perhaps a surprise in last place — Gary Cowan of Canada, U.S. Champion in 1966 and 1971.

Just food for thought, mind you.

26. Reflections at Newport, *Rhode Island, scene of the first U.S. Open in 1895*

It is not intentionally sacrilegious to describe the death of my boyhood idol Bobby Jones in December 1971 as a merciful release.

I treasure a letter from him thanking me for my enthusiastic review of his great instructional book, *Bobby Jones on Golf*, when it was first published in England in 1968. But the obviously tortured signature told fully a story I knew only too well, that Jones's body had been almost finally destroyed by the mysterious spinal ailment that made a misery of the last third of his life. Ironically, it left his magnificent brain intact.

I first met Jones in 1958 when he captained the American team from a wheelchair or cart in the first Eisenhower Trophy meeting at St. Andrews. Thirty-seven years previously, as a slip of a lad playing in his first Open championship on the Old Course, Jones had torn up his card during his third round, teed up his ball, and driven it far into the River Eden. But during that momentous week, he became a freeman of a town in which he was revered at a ceremony that for sheer emotion drained everyone present. Jones's daughter later said, "I'll never forget Dad, how he got up on that stage and up to the lectern with his two walking sticks. He was determined to do it without any help. It was painful to watch him. I thought he'd never make it, but he did. He had worked hard on that speech of acceptance, and it was beautiful. It became quite emotional at the end, and then he and the provost were seated in a golf cart and they drove down the aisle through the hall. People were crying and reaching out to touch him, and to touch even us — my mother, my brother, and me. I felt like the queen of England. Then almost in unison, purely spur of the moment, I think, they began singing 'Will Ye No' Come Back Again?' well knowing that he never would."

Bernard Darwin, in the foreword to the best book about the great man, *The Bobby Jones Story*, by O. B. Keeler and Grantland Rice, wrote of Jones's famous victory in the Open of 1930 at Hoylake: "I was writing in the room where he was waiting to know if he had won. He was utterly exhausted and had to hold his glass in two hands lest the good liquor be spilt. All he could say was that he would never, never do it again. Golf had always taken a prodigious toll and now I thought it had taken too great a one."

Jones retired from serious competition later that same year at the age of 28, having accomplished the astonishing and unrepeatable feat of winning the Open and Amateur championships of both Britain and America in a single season. Between 1923 and 1930 — after that seven-year-long battle against his temperament — Jones won 13 major national titles.

In 1929, when Jones won the U.S. Open after a play-off against Al Espinosa, Keeler, his personal biographer and friend from his native Atlanta, wrote critically that Jones had played only 10 rounds of golf in the previous six months — "not enough practice for a national Open, and that accounted for his collapse in the fourth round." On this occasion Jones led Espinosa by six shots with six holes to play and yet was finally forced to hole an historic 12-foot putt to tie, having bunkered his second shot in front of the eighteenth green on the West Course at Winged Foot.

If Jones and Jack Nicklaus are to be compared, which is ridiculous but inevitable, it is the former's purely natural talent for the game that would always put him ahead in my book. The argument often put forward in favor of Nicklaus is a singularly ignorant one — namely that the competition today is much tougher. Four of Jones's greatest rivals — Walter Hagen, Gene Sarazen, Jim Barnes and Tommy Armour — all won both the U.S. and British Opens and the U.S. PGA Championships, hardly a lightweight achievement.

Jones played so many great and crucial golf shots that to try to pick out the greatest he ever struck is another invidious task. Most would plump for his second shot at the seventeenth hole at Royal Lytham in the last round of the 1926 Open — the first of his three victories — which has been immortalized by the plaque placed in the bunker at the angle of the dogleg. Jones, playing alongside

Al Watrous, his only rival, took the ball clean and hit it some 170 yards to the hidden green. As Darwin, who saw the shot, commented, "A teaspoonful of sand could have ruined it."

Jones himself chose the 120-yard bunker shot straight into the hole at the 427-yards fourth at the first round of the Amateur Championship of 1930. This put him three-up against an unknown Nottingham coal miner, Sid Roper, after a start of 3, 4, 3, 2. Jones had been told that Roper was a level fives scorer. In fact, Roper threw 15 fours and only one five at his illustrious opponent, and went down by 3 and 2.

The worst hole Jones ever played came about at Hoylake in the Open a month later. Jones had been reaching the green regularly at the 482-yard eighth hole with driver and spoon. In the last round he pulled his second shot pin-high but in no apparent trouble. Jones then proceeded to take five more shots to get down.

As he described it, "It was the most inexcusable hole I ever played." To have won after such a disaster was a measure of Jones's character. I quote Keeler's final comment in his book on that subject when the "grand slam" had been achieved, since no one knew Jones better.

"And now it was goodbye to golf. And I could still say what I had said to people all over the world — they could see for themselves if he was a golfer, but I could tell them that he was much finer a young man than he was a golfer. His great personality was paralleled only by his inimitable swing. Wholly lacking in affectation, modest to the degree of shyness, generous and thoughtful of his opponents, it is not likely that his equal will come again."

27. A "Single" on Gullane #1, *Scotland.*
At Gullane one comes upon strange-looking obstacles that might be thought of as some sort of impediment; that's exactly what they are — tank traps put there to protect the coast of Scotland during World War II.

28. The Locker

46

If ever a great golfer came "made for television" it was Gene Sarazen. Alas, "The Squire" arrived too early to really impress his startling charisma on the small screen, except perhaps as occasional co-host with the late, similarly appealing Jimmy Demaret on Shell's "Wonderful World of Golf" filmed matches.

To those fortunate enough, however, to have witnessed the BBC's coverage of his astonishing hole in one at the "Postage Stamp," Royal Troon's beguilingly beautiful but viciously dangerous par-three, 126-yard eighth hole, during the 1973 Open Championship, there have been few, if any, more dramatic moments in the televised history of the game. Sarazen, in the twilight of his distinguished career, was 71 years of age at the time. And to the astonishment of the few spectators present in the same area the following day, Sarazen calmly holed out from a deep greenside bunker for a two that was scarcely less theatrical.

Offshore at North Berwick

What a crying shame it is that television cameras were not around when Sarazen recorded his incredible albatross, or double-eagle two, at Augusta National's par-five fifteenth hole that enabled him to catch Craig Wood and go on to win the 1935 Masters tournament, strangely his last championship victory.

Sarazen had virtually passed from contention when he reached the fifteenth tee in the final round. Wood was already the leader in the clubhouse with a total of 282, and Gene knew he required three birdies himself to tie. In those days, the fifteenth hole measured 485 yards and, after a good drive, Sarazen was 220 yards from the flag. When his spoon shot went into the cup, he picked up the three strokes he required, and he safely parred the last three holes. Not surprisingly, Sarazen retained his momentum the following day to win the 36-hole playoff by five shots, scoring 144 to Wood's 149.

Gene always played golf at almost a gallop, like his Scottish contemporary George Duncan, who made all his decisions about every shot long before he reached his ball. Sarazen was openly and mercilessly critical of slow players such as Ben Hogan, Dr. Cary Middlecoff, and even young Jack Nicklaus. In 1947, Gene and George Fazio were first off the tee in the final round of the Masters, and they holed the course in one hour, 57 minutes. Sarazen scored 70. Now that's my kind of player!

Bobby Jones, who like Walter Hagen was one of Sarazen's two chief rivals in the 1930s, said of Gene, "Sarazen has ever been the impatient, headlong player who went for everything in the hope of feeling the timely touch of inspiration. When the wand touches him, he is likely to win in a great finish as he did at Fresh Meadow (U.S. Open, 1932) and Skokie (U.S. Open, 1922), or in a parade as he did at Prince's (Sandwich, Kent, England, Open, 1932), but if it touch him not throughout the four rounds, the boldness of his play leaves no middle ground. When he is in the right mood, he is probably the greatest scorer in the game, possibly that the game has ever seen."

Praise, indeed, for one who was mounting dramatic charges when Arnold Palmer, later noted for his charges, was still in short pants.

One of the most effective charges of all time was Sarazen's at Fresh Meadow on Long Island in the U.S. Open of 1932. Gene had been professional at the club between 1925 and 1930, and knew its pitfalls intimately. The odds appeared stacked against him. Only Jones had previously won both the British and U.S. Opens in a single year, and Sarazen came to a course in which he had never bettered 67 in hundreds of relaxed games there, fresh from victory in the British Open.

In two practice rounds with Jones, Sarazen revealed his game plan to play ultraconservatively rather than in his normal swash-buckling, attacking style, and Jones was frankly amazed. The result was two scrappy opening rounds of 74 and 76.

When Sarazen came to the ninth tee in his third round, he was eight strokes behind the leaders and disgusted enough with himself to throw caution, so alien to his nature, to the wind. He hit a seven-iron shot at the 143-yard ninth hole 12 feet from the cup, rammed in the putt, and became inspired. Home in 32 shots for a round of 70, Sarazen blazed through his final round in 66 strokes to win his second U.S. Open title by three from Phil Perkins and Bobby Cruickshank. Sarazen had played his last 28 holes in exactly 100 strokes . . . phenomenal.

Gene's first U.S. Open victory at Skokie in 1922 was scarcely less dramatic, in that he was a 20-year-old virtually unknown ex-caddie in his first job as a full professional; he had won but one tournament, the New Orleans Open in the winter of 1921-22. One well-established star even refused to play a practice round with Sarazen. But Gene had a premonition that he could win, and so he put in very long hours of practice. Rounds of 72 and 73 kept him in a position to challenge, but a third of 75 —

W hen Gene Sarazen was asked at one of his last serious Masters participations whom he was playing with the next day, he commented, "Tomorrow, an old legend tees off with a new legend, Arnold Palmer."

including eight fives — put him five shots adrift of Jones and Wild Bill Melhorn as he went out early for his final round in the company of Johnny Farrell.

After reaching the green in two excellent shots at the 450-yard third hole, he told Farrell, "I might as well go for everything now." Sarazen holed out from 40 feet. At the short par-four fourth hole he was 25 feet from the cup in two and said, "I'll give this one a chance too, Johnny," as he returned to his ball after carefully lining up the putt. It, too, went in, and Sarazen was away, attacking every hole until he reached the par-five eighteenth needing a birdie for 68 and a total of 288. He calmly lashed a second driver shot from the fairway to the

fringe of the green, two-putted, and settled down with a big black cigar as all his illustrious rivals were to fall by the wayside.

The press went berserk over their latest Cinderella story, and when Sarazen won the first of his PGA titles shortly afterward, the innocently arrogant youth challenged Walter Hagen to a 72-hole match for the unofficial "Championship of the World," and beat him by 3 and 2. As Herbert Warren Wind wrote in *The Story of American Golf*, "Only Gene Sarazen, who was as intrinsically cocky as Hagen and could fight fire with fire, was able to stand up to him in man-to-man combat."

But although Sarazen was to retain his PGA title in 1923, he was to disappear from view as a frequent winner just as quickly as he had emerged. Undoubtedly because of his humble origins, Gene was anxious to cash in on his success. He went on a bewilderingly busy expedition tour, endorsed golf clubs, balls, and most anything else. He set up a golfing correspondence course, made instructional films, and published a book. One of his most interesting contributions to the game was his invention of the sand wedge for the Wilson Company; the new club helped him to banish what he had regarded as a chink in his armor — bunker play.

But perhaps most disastrous of all, he started to dissect his own swing that had come so naturally. He gratefully accepted all advice as he struggled to regain his lost form.

Sarazen's great friend and rival Hagen, who had won the British Open in 1922 and 1924, told Gene on the ocean liner from America to Britain for the 1932 Open that he needed a good caddie if he was to win the title he now craved

29. The "Postage Stamp" at Troon, *Scotland, 8th hole*

30. Rain Gear

more than any other. Hagen went still further. He offered Sarazen his own expert local caddie, Skip Daniels, who had guided Hagen to victory at Royal St. George's in 1922, for the princely sum of $200!

Although frail and well into his sixties, Daniels was everything that Hagen had said he would be. Alas, he and Sarazen had only one moment of dissension, and it was Gene's impatient impetuosity in overruling his caddie that was to cost him the championship. In the second round, Sarazen hooked his drive away from the out-of-bounds fence into deep rough at the 520-yard fourteenth, known as "Suez Canal." Daniels advised an iron club. Sarazen brushed his caddie away, lashed abortively at his ball twice with his spoon, took seven, and lost to Hagen with irritating irony by two shots.

In 1932 Sarazen scorned Daniels, now considerably feebler in health, in favor of a youngster. But the new combination never hit it off, and Sarazen's form in practice was consequently miserable. Reason eventually prevailed, however. In desperation Sarazen fired the youth and gave his bag to Daniels. The rest is history.

Sarazen won going away by five shots with a record aggregate of 283 that stood the test of time until Bobby Locke won the event with a total of 279 at Troon in 1950. Poor Daniels died shortly after the 1932 Open. As ever, Sarazen's unconscious flair for the dramatic always seemed to lend a fictional aspect to his entire career.

Australian Peter Thomson, fabled five-time winner of the British Open, always has been fascinating to me because of his many-faceted character, the intellectual leanings that make him so different from the average, blinkered golf professional whose life revolves around airports, golf courses, motels, and courtesy cars. For instance, during the early '60s, Thomson devoted much of his time to pioneering an Asian circuit, having had a dream of a world circuit as an alternative, or complement to the American tour. He

"The Open" Trophy

became deeply involved in the administration of the Australian PGA and in the constant battle against the payment of huge sums of appearance money to imported star performers.

Nor were politics ever far from Thomson's thoughts. He says, "I had always been vitally interested in politics since my early days of sitting at the feet of Sir Robert Menzies, the greatest politician Australia ever produced — and I include the present bunch." In 1982 he offered himself for public office in the Victorian State election and lost by a narrow four percent.

Thomson has been a somewhat controversial figure in golf politics as well, having been accused on more than one occasion in the last 30 years of being decidedly anti-American. "It is just not true that I dislike Americans. But as their rival in golf, I believe in keeping them at arm's length. I don't want to get any closer to men who know I am out to beat them, just as they are anxious to hammer me into the ground. Such a relationship would be an artificial and phoney one and detrimental to my mental attitude.

"I learned to play the American game between 1951 and 1960, and it revolted me. I have always regarded the bounce of the ball as the third dimension in golf, but the ball is not allowed to bounce in America. It is sickening to see the game reduced to something like archery or darts.

"Golf only becomes really difficult and challenging on hard courses. It is then that skill, not strength, counts for everything. If the ground is allowed to become firm by the natural processes of the weather, then the ball will bounce as it should and as it was intended to do. I turned my back on America when I saw them designing and constructing heavily watered courses over 7,000 yards long.

"It's only a matter of time before some American manager comes up with a gorilla who stands six feet, eight inches tall and has been trained to wallop the ball 400 yards. Then he'll win everything over there. Or perhaps they'll teach chimpanzees to play."

Before the 1959 tournament at Muirfield, Scotland, the British Open had reached its lowest ebb. The American challenge was minimal, consisting of an aging Johnny Bulla and sundry club professionals, and the format of playing two rounds on the final day, Friday, had become anachronistic. It was no longer crucial for British club professionals playing in the Open to be back in their shops prompt and early on Saturday morning.

Gary Player, the young South African recently come into his own, had breezed through the final round and led the tournament until he came to the par-four eighteenth hole. He made a complete hash of it, taking a double bogey.

Because in those days the leaders did not play last and the luck of the draw was a considerable factor in terms of weather conditions, there was a good chance that Player's two closest rivals, still on the course, could overtake him. Player was so convinced he had thrown away the title that he became inconsolable. He went to the little hut — very much like that occupied by sentries — adjacent to the eighteenth green to check and sign his scorecard. Player rested his head in his hands and wept openly and profusely for what seemed an eternity before signing and handing over his card. His guide and mentor, George Blumberg, then took Player and his wife back to their hotel room.

As the afternoon wore on, it became apparent that neither the elegant Belgian, Flory van Donck, nor English-born club professional Fred Bullock, whose daughter pulled his clubs on a trolley throughout the championship, could overtake Player. So the search for the missing Player became frantic. Eventually, he was reached by telephone, asleep in his hotel room, and told to get back to the club as soon as possible for the presentation. Player's joy, relief, and sense of triumph were complete as he became the British Open's youngest champion at age 23.

The following year at St. Andrews in the Centenary Open, Arnold Palmer made his first appearance to the delight of the crowd. Jack Nicklaus followed him in 1962, and a golden era dawned for the British Open.

When Palmer returned for the 1961 Open at Royal Birkdale, not even the tempest that washed out play and flattened all the tents could defy him and his iron resolve. No one present will ever forget the awesome, monstrous stroke Palmer fashioned from the willow scrub into the teeth of the gale to the plateau green at the sixteenth hole in the final round that is to this day commemorated by a brass plaque. Dai Rees, who was clinging to Palmer's heels like the proverbial Welsh terrier, was finally subdued, as were the elements, by Palmer's implacable strength of character.

At Old Troon in 1962, Palmer was to extract sweet revenge on the unfortunate Kel Nagle of Australia, winner of the Centenary Open, who played alongside him throughout the final day and was forced to look on helplessly as Palmer pulled inexorably away from him to win by nine shots. In those three short years Palmer had restored the prestige of the championship, and by his continuing support, and that of Nicklaus, Player, Trevino, and company had assured its place in the "big four" for the foreseeable future.

I shall never forget the tears Nicklaus shed after he had dropped strokes to par at two of the last four holes at Royal Lytham in the 1963 Open, when the increased adrenaline flow betrayed him twice into going through the green into virtually unplayable lies. Nor the tears he, and practically everyone else present, shed at Hoylake in 1967 when, after 20 years of valiant striving and narrow failure, we watched the beloved Argentinian Roberto de Vicenzo come down the eighteenth fairway finally to claim his British Open title — at Nicklaus's expense.

31. Royal Lytham, *England*

32. Going to the Co-op, *Ireland*

The late Henry Longhurst was the most brilliant television announcer I have ever had the pleasure to hear. In the early days of televised golf on BBC-TV in Great Britain, Henry would be virtually alone at the microphone for much of the day — with no commercial breaks — and I scarcely, if ever, heard him repeat himself or say anything remotely redundant.

One day in July 1958 stands out in my mind as the best possible example of Longhurst's wit and wisdom. The 36-hole play-off for the British Open between Peter Thomson of Australia, winner in 1954, 1955, and 1956 and second in 1957, and the then young Welsh giant Dave Thomas had been less one-sided than most had forecast. Thomson (68) led Thomas (69) narrowly at lunch at Royal Lytham and St. Anne's. But after the break Thomson pulled inexorably away from the great British hope to win by four shots, round in 71 to Thomas's 74.

Never at a loss for words, Longhurst was as near to struggling as I ever heard him in mid-afternoon, by which time the eventual result had become almost a foregone conclusion.

With great aplomb, Henry seized on a diversion in the shape of one of the last of British Rail's steam locomotives, belching forth clouds of steam and billowing dark smoke as it tugged six incredibly dirty and decrepit passenger coaches out of the local station close by the golf course. Thomson and Thomas had just driven at the par-five eleventh hole and were walking at the time.

"If our cameraman can pan a little left," Henry intoned, "you fortunate people in your armchairs at home will be able to feast your eyes on one of the last, ill-fated Leviathans of the once formidable British rail system, shortly to be sent without

ceremony to the knacker's yard and replaced by one of those infernal, unromantic and evil-smelling diesels. Oh! The shame of it all. Ah! Now you can see this wonderful giant, better known to train buffs as a 4-6-2. Isn't that a magnificent sight? Take it all in while you can, because you are watching the splendor of a dying breed, even if she is condemned to pulling the 4:10 P.M. stopping train from Lytham North to Manchester Central, calling at. . . ." And Longhurst proceeded to name all the stations at which this train would stop along its route. That alone was a virtuoso performance.

Henry went on as he warmed to the task: "You can see the sweat on the brow of the fireman and the coal dust on his strong hands and forearms as he shovels fuel into the mouth of the monster, which has such a relentless appetite. Now if our cameraman can pan a little right we can read the number on the tender of this noble beast. Let me see now — two, three, two, four, four, three, four. My word! If only our man Thomas could reel off figures like those over the next few holes we might have a contest yet. Oh, by the way, neither player has reached the green with his second shot."

Henry Longhurst was, indeed, a master.

The immortal Bernard Darwin wrote in 1910 of Royal St. George's Golf Club, Sandwich, Kent, in his marvelous tome *The Golf Courses of the British Isles* with some vehemence: "Confound their politics, one feels disposed to say, frustrate their knavish tricks! Why do they want to alter this adorable place? I know they are perfectly right, and I have even agreed with them that this is a blind shot and that an indefensively bad hole,

> Rumored retort from an oldtime caddy at Prestwick when his "bag" commented upon seeing the tenth hole "Arran" for the first time:
> "How long is this hole?"
> "It'll take three fine shots to get home in two."

but what does it all matter? This is perfect bliss."

When I first looked at Frank Pennink's plans for the alterations to this great links some years ago, I was completely out of sympathy with Darwin's sentiments. The blind par-three third hole of 228 yards, known aptly as Sahara, was a ridiculous anachronism, a total lottery.

On more than one occasion in the beloved Halford Hewitt tournament — still the most enjoyable event in which I have ever participated — I missed the invisible green with what I thought had been a well nigh perfect shot. On another it had been embarrassing to find that my ball had somehow made its way onto the putting surface when I imagined I had hit it so thin it must hang up somewhere in a vilely unplayable spot in the sandhills, and rightly so.

One just had to stand up on the tee, aim at the marker post, flail away and hope for the best. Such a hole has no place in modern golf, and it was duly replaced by Pennink's splendid creation, a thoroughly visible 216-yard hole played from an elevated tee over the desert to a plateau green nestling among the dunes, with a deceptive swale in front of it.

Just as surely, the absurdly blind drive over the monster dunes at the par-four, 466-yard fourth hole was quite out of character with the generally held concepts of modern golf architecture. I was never unfortunate enough to tangle with the bigger of the two bunkers set in the face of this formidable mountain, but I do remember taking three to get out of the smaller pit.

And, I still occasionally awaken sweating profusely at the childhood memory of a teen-aged opponent tumbling from top to bottom of the Himalaya bunker at St. Enodoc Golf Club in rural Cornwall, a fate that could easily befall a victim of the bigger bunker at Royal St. George's fourth. Pennink sensibly moved the tee to the left so that the massive dune was removed from the direct line of fire, and the flagstick can be seen beckoning in the distance perilously close by the out-of-bounds fence behind the green.

If Royal St. George's was to host its first Open Championship since Bobby Locke's first of four victories was recorded there in 1949, the course couldn't possibly have three par threes on the outward half and only one on the way home, the sixteenth, where Tony Jacklin holed in one to signal his arrival in the big time in the 1967 Dunlop Masters. The eighth hole, known as Hades, was probably the least distinguished of the three, especially once the third had been "cleaned up," so it had to go.

Pennink replaced it with a neat par four and the old eleventh, which could be a beast of a par four, was replaced by a par three. The other significant change was to lengthen the second hole by some 50 yards to 391 to bring back into play the two cross bunkers that used to catch more than their share of tee shots in the days of the "gutty."

All these changes seemed to be absolutely logical at the time, and there is little doubt that Royal St. George's is now a better test of modern-era golf. But is it necessarily a better course? Is there any good reason why a great old course shouldn't have a blind par three like the Himalayas at Prestwick or the Dell at Lahinch? And does it matter a damn whether there are three par threes in one half and but one in the other just because the Open Championship was coming to town? The holes that have gone or have been "improved" were a part of history.

Has anyone suggested that the Mona Lisa needs makeup? I make the point because some of us who respect and admire the work of the great Scottish architect Donald Ross in the United States have been appalled at the efforts to improve and update his brilliant creations, most notably Oak Hill in Rochester, New York, venue of the 1980 U.S. PGA Championship. There it was that one of the best par fours in the world was summarily plowed up and replaced by one totally out of character, as is another, the newly created par-three fifteenth.

Should we be fooling with our golfing heritage, or should the British links, monuments to a wiser age, remain just that?

When I was much younger and doubtless less tradition conscious, I made a heretical suggestion that the first and eighteenth holes at St. Andrews could be immeasurably improved by extending the Swilcan Burn to run between them into a pond created by flooding the Valley of Sin. I beg forgiveness.

33. Over the Gorse, *Royal County Down, Newcastle, Northern Ireland*

Not so long ago I was asked to select "the best 18 holes of golf in Great Britain and Ireland." Although a consensus would be impossible and any list would certainly exclude some of the finest holes in the world, I accepted the challenge.

The terms of reference were simple enough: the number of the hole chosen from any course had to correspond to its position in the eclectic collection, so the seventeenth or Road Hole at St. Andrews had to be my seventeenth. I decided on the fashionable par of 72 to include four par-five holes and four par threes. It was my intention to include two par threes of close to or over 200 yards in length, and two hopefully much shorter.

To make the task easier, I limited my selection to holes drawn from those courses that have hosted major championships, with one notable exception, that wonderful Irish gem, Ballybunion. I also tried to come up with holes that are both aesthetically pleasing and at the same time testing enough in a golfing sense for ordinary mortals.

My idea of the perfect opening hole is a comparatively straight par-four of medium length and no great difficulty, to allow the humblest hacker to collect his thoughts and loosen his joints. In case of the last-minute arrival who has had no time or facilities to hit practice balls — and why are there so many of us arrogant enough to do this on a regular basis? — we shall not be too hard on him, even if he deserves punishing.

The first hole at Royal St. George's, Kent, with its wide and gently rolling fairway, at 415 yards in length is my idea of a perfect pipe-opener, with just a cross bunker to menace the second shot to a generous green.

But the second hole, taken from Royal Lytham and St. Anne's, is much more demanding, although only five yards longer at 420, with the railway and out of bounds all the way down the right. Two bunkers strategically placed to the left of the fairway victimize those who shy away too cautiously in that direction. The narrow entrance to the green is heavily bunkered to the left and right.

Historic Old Prestwick may be an anachronism in terms of modern equipment and design, but its third hole, a par five of 482 yards, is dominated at the angle of the dogleg to the right by the massive Cardinal bunker running the full width of the fairway, and buttressed in front by a forbidding wall of railway ties.

The fourth hole is our first par three, the 211-yard fourth at Royal County Down, which, with the gorse in full bloom, is almost too beautiful for words, with the small town of Newcastle and the Mountains of Mourne beyond as a breathtaking backdrop. No fewer than 10 bunkers defend the green.

The elevated tee at the 410-yard fifth hole at Sunningdale Old offers a glorious view over a huge expanse of heather to a fairway dominated by two bunkers to the right, impenetrable woodland to the left, and thick rough on both sides. The green is protected in front by a small pond and four greenside bunkers. Like the whole course, the fifth here is enchanting rather than brutal.

But brutal is a fair way to describe the 469-yard sixth hole at Royal Birkdale. A big cross bunker is set into a ridge of dunes at the angle of the dogleg to the right, which is an impossible carry from the tee for the mere hacker with the prevailing wind in his face. Any tee shot hit too far to the right produces a second shot blocked out by towering sandhills. The green nestles into a horseshoe of these menacing, scrub-covered monsters with three attendant bunkers.

Because I believe every course should have at least one par four of less than 400 yards, and preferably a really short one that presents several alternative methods of approach, I included the seventh hole of the Old Course at St. Andrews, 372 yards long, with its almost blind drive and a veritable sea of gorse to trap a push or slice from the tee. The green, shared with the par-three eleventh, has a huge bunker in front. This is really our only let-up hole on the outward half.

But there is nothing benign, except its length, about the fabled Postage Stamp eighth hole at Royal Troon, only 126 yards long but with a tiny green surrounded

34. Westport, *Ireland*

35. Checking the Distance, *Ballybunion, Ireland*

by five deeply intimidating bunkers and set so appealingly in a sort of saddle of dune. In my opinion, this hole at Troon, the 107-yard seventh hole at Pebble Beach, and the 139-yard fifteenth at Cypress Point are the three best short par threes in the world — each less than 150 yards long.

Because a par five was required to complete the outward half, I had no hesitation in choosing the dangerously narrow 495-yard ninth hole at Muirfield over the splendid Lighthouse hole, the bleak and rugged 475-yard par-four ninth at Turnberry, one of the world's most photographed holes. Muirfield's ninth poses its own myriad problems, with a tiny driving area to the right of a strategically placed fairway bunker. Now the golfer has to face a dauntingly difficult second shot to stay away from a gaggle of bunkers to the right and well short of the green, which means that he is aiming straight at the five-foot-high gray stone wall running the entire length of the hole, over which is out of bounds to the left perilously close to the green. Many are the second and third shots that have floated fatally over that dreaded wall.

So our outward half of par 36 measures just 3,399 yards, a very reasonable distance for ordinary mortals but testing enough for the best.

If you questioned my sanity in abandoning Turnberry's ninth, rest assured it was only because I regard the brilliant 460-yard tenth hole every bit its equal — less rugged maybe, but beguilingly beautiful. One stands on the high tee just beyond the ruins of Robert the Bruce's castle and plays literally down the shoreline as it curves left along the beach, the World War I monument high atop the dunes to the right. A big bunker containing a grassy island dominates the fairway as one approaches the green, and another at greenside catches all but the resolute second shot.

The 443-yard eleventh hole at Bally-bunion swoops down to the very edge of the Atlantic to the right, with the twin threat of maybe the biggest sandhills in Ireland to the left. Simply put, this noble and dramatic hole is a memorable example of all that is best in links golf.

The twelfth hole at Royal Lytham is the only par three on that course's inward half, and at 189 yards presents the most difficult shot into any of the 18 greens on this superbly balanced test of golf. The tee is completely protected from the prevailing left-to-right wind by a dense wood of wind-gnarled trees, so that the tee shot must be held up against it if the raised green is to receive the ball kindly, rather than the deep bunkers to the left and at its right front. Any tee shot overhit or drifting on the prevailing wind is out of bounds into the road in a heartbeat.

At the 426-yard thirteenth hole at Royal Portcawl in South Wales, one's drive is struck up to the highest point on the course. The views are as breathtaking as they are dismal at Royal Lytham, but that tee shot to a very narrow fairway is exposed to the full force of the prevailing westerly winds. From the magnificent vantage point at the crest of the hill, the hole swings abruptly left and down to a well-guarded green with the shimmering sea beyond, while most of the holes around the great basin of the course are plainly visible.

The 567-yard fourteenth hole on the Old Course at St. Andrews is probably the greatest par five in the British Isles, if not the whole world, if only for the infinite variety of routes by which one can travel to the green in the ever changing conditions. The drive must be placed between the out-of-bounds wall on the right and the cluster of five "Beardies" bunkers to the left. From there only the brave and longest of hitters will attempt to carry the yawning expanse of Hell Bunker. Either from the left or right of this cavernous hazard, the third shot is a fiendishly treacherous one over a steep bank from which the green slopes away from the player.

Who says one cannot have consecutive par fives? Four of the last six holes at Royal Birkdale measure over 500 yards, but easily the most testing of the four is the 542-yard fifteenth, usually played into the teeth of the prevailing wind. The drive must be very accurate to avoid three deep bunkers in echelon down the left and deep rough to the right. No fewer than eight bunkers must be carried by those players whose drives have afforded them the chance of carrying the last three and perhaps reaching the green, which is protected by yet three more bunkers, scrub, and wind-battered bushes on three sides.

Carnoustie's 235-yard sixteenth hole is part of the most demanding finish of any of the great British links, a brutally long and demanding tee shot into the tiniest of gaps between two bunkers to the left and four to the right of a narrow sliver of a green. This tee shot to me is as intimidating as that presented by the sixteenth at Cypress Point, albeit with no cliffs or Pacific Ocean with which to contend.

There are many marvelous seventeenth holes around Great Britain and Ireland, but it came down to a final choice between the Road Hole at St. Andrews and the 413-yard seventeenth at Royal Lytham, from one of whose left-hand fairway bunkers Bobby Jones picked clean his 175-yard second shot with his hickory-shafted mashie in the final round of the 1926 Open. Al Watrous, with whom Jones was tied for the lead, was already on the green in two shots. When Jones's ball pulled up much closer to the hole after the miraculous recovery, the unfortunate Watrous understandably fatally three-putted, and then he bunkered his second shot at the last to assure Jones of

victory. The famous plaque marks the spot from which this most courageous and historic shot was played.

A similar plaque marks a spot in the virtually impenetrable willow scrub to the right of the fifteenth (a 381-yard hole in the 1961 Open that is now the 404-yard sixteenth) at Royal Birkdale. It was from this unenviable position that eventual Open winner Arnold Palmer played his heroic second shot, strong-arming his ball with his six-iron some 145 yards into a gale onto an exposed plateau green heavily guarded by bunkers. The ball stopped 15 feet from the flagstick. If I hadn't been standing close by at the time, I would never have believed it. This is probably a heretical statement to those in the corridors of power at "headquarters," but I prefer the seventeenth at Royal Lytham to St. Andrews' Road Hole because I believe the latter is so severe it borders on the unfair. Certainly it is by far the tougher of the two.

The eighteenth hole at Muirfield, 447 yards long, is as typically fair as is the whole course. Bluntly put, what you see from the tee is what you get — all that is required of a truly wonderful last hole. A tight drive must pitch between three bunkers left and one big one to the right. Similarly, the second shot leaves no margin for error as it is hit over two bunkers to a narrow target whose embracing bunkers left and right are deep and pitilessly penal.

Our inward half thus measures 3,773 yards, tough enough for anybody. Our total eclectic course yardage measures 7,172 yards, par 72, and will probably come under immediate and heavy fire from spirited critics.

36. Cypress Point, *California*

37. The 4th at Baltusrol, *New Jersey*

Putting together an eclectic collection of what I consider the best 18 holes in America was a truly agonizing business, in that so many wonderful holes had to be left out, particularly to achieve a balance of four par threes and par fives and 10 par fours, par 72 (36-36).

If you agree that a first hole should not be too hard on its victims, then there is nothing better in America than the 355-yard first hole on the East course at Merion Golf Club in Ardmore, Pennsylvania, a dogleg to the right round a grove of evergreens, with three bunkers in line down the right and two to the left of a most generous fairway. Another bunker running across most of the fairway's width precludes any attempt to run the ball onto the green, which is both narrow and heavily bunkered on both sides and even to the rear. In short, this is the best-designed opening hole I have seen, a brilliant short par four.

An immediate change of pace is posed at the 555-yard second hole at Peachtree Golf Club in north Atlanta, Georgia, the brainchild of Bobby Jones and designed by Robert Trent Jones. The hole is completely bunkerless but the second shot, if attempted by a mere hacker — rather than a modest lay-up — presents an awesome carry over a stream and lake, which also protects the right side of the green. Quite simply, a fine hole of this difficulty does not require bunkers.

My third hole is one of the finest at Shinnecock Hills Golf Club, Southampton, Long Island, the 454-yard third. The drive must carry an expanse of rough and three bunkers and not be allowed to drift into another, a big one to the right with a rough grass island in the center. The second shot is also played uphill and is similarly menaced by three bunkers in line down the right, while

38. Shinnecock Hills Clubhouse, *Southampton, New York*

the generous green is bunkered left and right.

The 194-yard fourth hole at Baltusrol Country Club in Springfield, New Jersey, demands a heroic stroke — all carry over a lake to a wide but shallow green protected in front by a forbidding stone wall and a bunker to the left. Guarding the rear of the green are three more bunkers to catch those who overclub in fear of the water. Those who do find any of those bunkers will find the lake staring them in the eye as they play down a considerable slope out of the sand.

My next choice is the 459-yard fifth hole at Colonial Country Club in Fort Worth, Texas — a most claustrophobic dogleg to the right with the Trinity River lurking behind the trees on the right from tee to green.

The sixth hole at Seminole Golf Club in Palm Beach, Florida, designed by Donald Ross, measures but 388 yards. Yet it is distinguished — as is the whole course — by its profusion of bunkers, close to 200 of them. The tee shot here must carry as much as you dare of a monstrous line of bunkers down the left-hand side. And if you succeed in finding the fairway, the second shot must be struck over another set of four huge bunkers, again set in echelon down the right. Two more bunkers guard the left-hand side of the pitilessly narrow green, and so there are 11 in all.

If there is a veritable sea of sand at Seminole, then Pine Valley Golf Club's 595-yard seventh hole in Clementon, New Jersey, boasts the biggest bunker in the world, the infamous "Hell's Half Acre," which actually measures one and a half acres and is liberally sprinkled with brush and scrub. The tee shot must

be less than 260 yards in length to avoid running into this terrifying hazard, the second shot must carry it, and the third must find a green that is literally an island surrounded by a moat of sand.

The 420-yard eighth hole at Prairie Dunes Country Club in Hutchinson, Kansas, is a dogleg to the right played slightly uphill over a succession of four dunes cutting across the fairway, the first at 165 yards from the tee, the last — almost 50 feet high — about 140 yards from the green. Four small bunkers speckled with yucca plants are placed to the right and short of the green, and another one to the left — a tremendous par four.

The 189-yard ninth hole on Doral Country Club's "Blue Monster" course in Miami, Florida, is set in the middle of the lake that separates it from the tenth and the renowned eighteenth holes, on a narrow peninsula. Like the fourth at Baltusrol, its carry measures some 180 yards over water, which also flanks the green on both sides — all or nothing. The outward half of my selection measures 3,603 yards, despite the presence of two parfours measuring under 400 yards.

The 190-yard tenth hole on the West course at Winged Foot Country Club in Mamaroneck, New York, is to me one of Arthur W. Tillinghast's most aesthetically pleasing masterpieces of design. It is played over a valley to a generously long and broad green flanked at front by two very deep kidney-shaped bunders set into the hillside. The out-of-bounds fence lurks 30 feet through the green, which slopes and undulates sharply down from back to front.

The eleventh hole at Merion is only 370 yards long, but it achieved lasting fame when Bobby Jones closed out Eugene Homans by 8 and 7 on its green in the 1930 U.S. Amateur championship final to complete the Grand Slam or Impregnable Quadrilateral. The tee shot is played down into the valley past decorative bunkers to left and right. A rocky creek passes across the fairway, divid-

U.S. Open

39. The 6th at Seminole, *Florida*

40. The 18th at Harbour Town, *Hilton Head Island, South Carolina*

ing into a tributary that bisects the fairway from that point onward in front of and to the right of a small raised green framed by tall trees and a bunker to its left. A seemingly innocent little par four has often become a disaster area.

The 456-yard twelfth hole at Southern Hills Country Club in Tulsa, Oklahoma, is one of several holes Ben Hogan has been quoted as calling the "greatest par-four in the United States." Trees and a gaping bunker at the inside angle of the dogleg to the left make for a very long and demanding second shot over one water hazard, with another to the right of the green, which is bunkered front, left, and behind.

By contrast, the 358-yard thirteenth hole at Harbour Town Links on Hilton Head Island off the shores of South Carolina presents the professionals with a long iron or fairway wood shot from the tee and a relatively short iron shot to the green. But both have to be played with minute accuracy, because two huge, overhanging trees intrude into the fairway from each side in the landing area from the tee, and the small, elevated green — shored up by railroad ties — is protected in front and on both sides by a single enormous bunker.

The 359-yard fourteenth hole at National Golf Links, set on Peconic Bay close to Southampton, Long Island, has a carry over water from the tee, while the road and beach beyond run the entire length of the hole to the right. Bunkers abound, four to the left of the fairway, two large ones down the right. The green is guarded by six more, while a great horseshoe of sand frames the almost circular green left, right, and rear.

Since the two outward par fives are virtually three-shot holes for ordinary mortals, the 500-yard fifteenth at Augusta National Golf Club in Georgia is perfectly placed to afford the bravest gamblers to go for its shallow sliver of green sitting beckoningly on a hill, with the sixteenth hole's own pond behind to punish the overly bold. Those who choose to lay up do so in the certain knowledge that they face one of the toughest third shots in all of golf, a wedge from a hanging lie to that raised green across the water. The solitary bunker on the hole to the right of the green is the bailout area.

41. The 15th at Harbour Town, *Hilton Head Island, South Carolina*

DUNBAR Golf Club

Because Merion is my favorite inland course in America and Cypress Point Golf Club on the Monterey Peninsula in California my favorite in all the world, I am not ashamed of choosing two holes from each. Cypress Point's 233-yard sixteenth and 375-yard seventeenth just happen to be two of my favorite three holes of all — the fifteenth at Cypress being the third.

The beauty of the sixteenth, apart from its incomparable setting, is that the golfer with no chance of making the carry over the raging Pacific Ocean from clifftop tee to green can play a modest tee shot away to the left and still hope to make a par with a pitch to and a putt on a green well guarded by four bunkers.

The seventeenth requires the tee shot across the clifftops to be placed far enough to the left so as not to involve a second shot over the grove of gnarled cypress trees close to the cliff at this dogleg to the right. The green is protected to the left and rear by massive bunkers.

Just down 17-Mile Drive at Pebble Beach Golf Links is the 540-yard eighteenth hole, inarguably the finest finishing hole in the world. The drive, almost always played with the wind at one's back, has to bite off as much of the shoreline as one dares. Pine trees, a huge bunker and the white out-of-bounds stakes beckon from the right. The lay-up second shot should hug the left as near as possible to the long bunker and its protective sea wall. In this way the big bunkers to the right and right front of the green are virtually taken out of play. One bunker to the left catches the errant pitch or anything badly hooked by a madman going for the green in two, and saves such a shot from the Pacific.

The inward half of my eclectic collection measures a trifling 3,361 yards for a total length of 6,964, par 72.

I was eating breakfast on Wednesday morning in the upstairs men's grill at Augusta National Golf Club in 1972 when a gentleman arrived on the scene in a high degree of panic. He asked loudly, "Does anyone here know a goddamn Limey who can speak halfway decent?"

My breakfast mate and friend Dan Jenkins proceeded to introduce me to Bill McPhail, then president of CBS-TV Sports, as "our man in London" because, in addition to my other British writing and broadcasting commitments at the time I was also stringing for both *Sports Illustrated* and *Time* magazine in Europe. It transpired that veteran broadcaster Henry Longhurst, my guide and mentor, had been taken to the university hospital in Augusta on suspicion of pneumonia. McPhail asked if I would stand in for Longhurst if required, and I readily agreed to do so.

But Henry made a miraculous recovery, so my Masters debut for CBS was put on hold until after I underwent a trial that August, live at the ill-fated L & M Matchplay championship at the Country Club of North Carolina. Passing that test, I was told that I would be part of the broadcast team for the next Masters tournament.

Thereby hangs a tale, however.

On arrival in Augusta from England in April 1973, McPhail explained that my Masters debut for the network was subject to the approval of tournament chairman Mr. Clifford Roberts, widely regarded as an iron-fisted tyrant.

When McPhail took me over to Mr. Roberts's cottage, it became immediately clear to me that the CBS brass were, to a man, terrified of the "old man," as they called him. McPhail could hardly wait to dart out of the door after introducing me to Mr. Roberts. The latter had thoughtfully ordered a pot of tea for me because, as he explained, "I have never known an Englishman turn down a cup of tea."

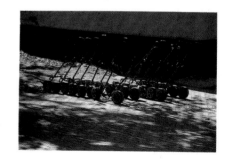

42. The Wall at Dunbar, Scotland. *Upon reaching the 18th hole at Dunbar, by the Firth of Forth in Scotland, the avid American golfer asked his host and Dunbar member, "How old is this marvelous wall?" "Very," replied the articulate Scot.*

I gulped down the fiery elixir in a state of fast-rising panic, whereupon Mr. Roberts said to me, "Young Wright, talk to me, boy." I asked him what I should talk about, and he replied gruffly that I could talk about anything I liked. So I rattled on for fully 30 seconds about my very early impressions of the Masters tournament.

"Stop!" Mr. Roberts held up his hand, and as he did so my heart sank into my boots. Had I blown it on the way to the starting gate? I asked myself.

You probably want to know why I stopped you so soon," intoned Mr. Roberts in his dry, deliberate way, and I mumbled feebly in the affirmative.

"Well, that McPhail sneaked one of yours past me last year; Scotsman, name of Bob Ferrier from Glasgow (a longtime Fleet Street colleague of mine). I listened to that joker every day, and from then until now I don't believe I understood a goddamn word he said! But you'll do. Have a good week."

With that I was dismissed to inform the petrified McPhail, lurking nearby, that I had been approved — to his immense and visible relief.

I later came to understand that the considerable influence of Mr. Roberts

43. The Gin Game

had a lot to do with my "promotion" the following year to the fifteenth hole, upon the television tower of which I have sat most gratefully every April since.

When I first began broadcasting the Masters tournament for CBS-TV in 1973, there were many forbidden words and phrases. Although I didn't know it at the time, my good friend-to-be Jack Whitaker was about to miss his eighth consecutive Masters broadcast, having been banned by tournament chairman Mr. Clifford Roberts for calling the gallery at the eighteenth hole a "mob."

I was later censured by the Masters Television and Radio Committee in itsannual critique of the broadcasts for referring to Lee Elder on his 1975 debut as "the leading black golfer" rather than "the leading golfer of his race." It was thus how hairs were split in those bad old days.

At that time the late Bill Kerr, then chairman of the above-mentioned committee, would give the broadcasting team from CBS a long annual dissertation on what could and could not be said by announcers. Year after year veteran announcer Henry Longhurst, who found Kerr, a stockbroker from San Diego, an insufferable bore, would mutter hardly sotto voce as the talk progressed, "I would never dream of venturing to the floor of the stock exchange to tell this wretched man how he should go about his business. Yet he dares to get up here every year and tell me how to broadcast golf." This is a very much cleaned-up version of the Longhurst condemnation. And, having delivered it, Henry would sleep through the rest of the proceedings.

44. Practice Green at Augusta

45. Flagman at Augusta

May 1990

Mr. Hord Hardin, Chairman

Masters Golf Tournament

Dear Mr. Hardin,

I have long admired your magnificent efforts to retain the traditions and heritage of excellence that Mr. Bobby Jones and Mr. Clifford Roberts established at Augusta National Golf Club in making the Masters tournament quite simply the best "major" of the four. I was fortunate enough to have been present when Mr. Jones was accorded the freedom of the burgh of St. Andrews, Scotland, during the week the Eisenhower Trophy competition was inaugurated in 1958, and I found his acceptance speech as moving as anything I have heard before or since.

I think it is extraordinarily generous of you to resist joining in the price gouging inflicted on the public at many PGA Tour stops and in much of Great Britain and Europe. And considering the price of your series badges ($90), it is little wonder that the scalpers have a field day! The patrons at the Masters seem to show their appreciation by being one of the most smartly attired, properly conducted audiences in all of professional golf. I love the color scheme throughout — cups, TV towers, bleachers, golf bags, towels, etc., all in Masters green. And I trust you regard it as the sincerest form of flattery that the Memorial and International tournaments strive so mightily to achieve a similar look and feel as you accomplish so successfully.

I also love the international flavor of the Masters, because such a magical ingredient has unfortunately become an endangered species on the increasingly isolationist PGA Tour, except on an occasional basis on the eve of the three majors played in the States. It is absolutely fitting that as a continuing homage to the memory of Mr. Jones, inarguably the greatest amateur golfer of all time in all the best sense of the word amateur, that you continue to encourage amateurs from both sides of the Atlantic to participate.

The vast sums of money you spend to beautify the course and its surroundings is admirably invested and partly explains why the Masters is watched by such a huge television audience worldwide. But it is perhaps the tireless attention to detail of all your various committees that contributes most in retaining the tournament's impeccable atmosphere as it performs the rites of spring.

I appreciate your concern about escalating prize money, and I know how you abhor the thought of the Masters becoming the "Pizza Hut Masters," as you once said, albeit tongue in cheek. Just as certainly I applaud your limitation of commercial breaks on Masters telecasts, and know you will never relax this wonderful arrangement that brings sharply into focus the continual interruptions of most other programs.

But I have blathered on as is my wont, Mr. Hardin, before really getting to the crux of the matter. Because I am an old sweat with 36 years' experience in the media business, I am deeply worried about what might happen when you eventually relinquish the reins at Augusta National. Greed is a sad fact of modern life, and I would hate for the next gentleman who assumes your mantle to be inordinately interested in using the Masters as a vehicle for profit rather than as a testament to golf.

The Masters has always stood head and shoulders above the other three majors, not to speak of the average Tour events, because of the Club's dogged resistance to the danger of allowing greed to interfere with integrity and the heritage established by Mr. Jones and Mr. Roberts, and nobly upheld by yourself.

So I am asking one favor of you, Mr. Hardin, on behalf of all who cherish this game. Before you hand over the Masters' mantle, please insist that every member of Augusta National Golf Club sign a sworn affidavit that he will never allow the Pizza Hut Masters or the Cadillac Masters or The Travelers' Masters or any other bloody commercialized Masters in his lifetime!

Best regards.

Ben Wright

P.S. Please hand on a copy of this letter to your successor,

Mr. Jack T. Stephens.

My assignment was to write an account of the ten most moving incidents I had witnessed in 38 years as a professional observer of the golf scene. I thought the task would be simple enough, but instead it proved extremely difficult: as I became embarrassingly aware of the rich experiences I have enjoyed.

The finish of the 1984 U.S. Open Championship at Winged Foot, New York, with its white towel (of surrender) waving incidents between winner Fuzzy Zoeller and Greg Norman, is on my list because it was such a splendid reminder, in these days of blatant commercialism in professional sport, that at least two great golfers can still regard their business as a game, even with so much at stake.

The U.S. Open rates only one other mention — Tony Jacklin's victory at Hazeltine National Golf Club in Chaska, Minnesota, in June 1970, because he became the first Briton to win the title in 50 years. But the reigning British Open champion won with such ease on such an unmemorable course that this triumph pales into insignificance when compared with his momentous triumph in the British Open of July 1969 at Royal Lytham. His perfect drive and splen-

didly played par four at the wickedly dangerous final hole — and the thunderous roar that greeted both — is indelibly printed on my memory. The years of humiliation since Max Faulkner had won the British title at Royal Portrush in 1951 faded away in this magical instant.

It seems almost sacrilegious for a Limey to accord the British Open only one other mention on a list to be compiled on strictly emotional terms. But I selected Roberto de Vicenzo's eventual British Open victory at Hoylake in 1967 after so many years of frustration, albeit frequently by the narrowest of margins.

Runner-up Jack Nicklaus, with whom I was standing at the green as Roberto strolled humbly down the eighteenth fairway to a tumultuous ovation, was

46. Junior Golfer

moved to copious tears, and he was far from being alone. The game has never known a more gentlemanly competitor, and the horrors of the 1968 Masters in Augusta, where he signed an incorrect scorecard to miss his chance for a playoff with Bob Goalby and possibly the championship, was easily my saddest moment in all those wonderful 35 years.

Nothing was more desperately exciting than our rare Walker Cup victory over the Americans at St. Andrews in 1971, with what seemed like hundreds of delirious Scotsmen hanging precariously from the chimney pots down the right side of the last fairway. Nothing except possibly the British and Irish Walker Cup victory, their first ever on foreign soil, in August 1989 at Peachtree Golf Club in Atlanta. It deserves mention because the series has remained so ridiculously one-sided since its inception in 1922. For the British and Irish to have won only thrice — in 1938, 1971, and 1989 — is truly ludicrous, but thankfully no one seems to care.

The Masters tournament has provided me with so much drama and excitement that it seems ridiculous to pass over the fabulously exciting finish at Augusta in 1975, when Johnny Miller came from behind, while Nicklaus and lifetime rival Tom Weiskopf traded punch for punch all afternoon. Finally, as everyone must remember, both Miller and Weiskopf missed their putts for birdies to tie Nicklaus at the 72nd hole.

But in purely emotional terms, I found myself more moved by Ben Crenshaw's overdue Masters victory in 1984, even more than I was moved by Nicklaus's astonishing sixth victory there in 1986 at the age of 46.

When I met "Gentle" Ben in the players' parking lot at Augusta National Golf Club on Monday morning following his victory, he shed a few tears when I asked him jokingly if he had stayed there all night.

It was as if he was so keen to savor his magic moment he could hardly bear to drag himself away from the stage on which the drama had been enacted. In fact, Ben told me he had had only one hour's sleep, and that only when he had finally cried his way to sleep shortly before dawn.

47. The Fabled 13th at Augusta

Crenshaw is perhaps revered even more in Britain than he is in the States for his complete reverence for the game's history, traditions, and integrity. At a time when many young players consider golf only as a lucrative business, Crenshaw still savors the GAME.

After his victory in the 1988 Doral Ryder Open, the fact that he had won $180,000 of the $1 million purse that day was of scant significance to him. The fact that he had played Doral's splendid "Blue Monster" in 66 strokes, without a single bogey, and had won a tremendous duel alongside his friend Ray Floyd that had come down to the final putt, now that was all important. That he had birdied the 18th hole, renowned as the toughest finishing hole on the tour, was icing on the cake, because he had disastrously hooked his drive into the lake the previous evening.

As Crenshaw told me in the first flush of victory, "Dick Wilson never built a finer course than this. And what makes winning even sweeter is that my name goes alongside the likes of Billy Casper, Doug Sanders, Jack Nicklaus, Lee Trevino, Tom Weiskopf, Ray Floyd, Lanny Wadkins, and the only three-time winner here, Andy Bean, on the trophy — pretty fast company."

One has come to expect respect for tradition from the older generation, players such as Palmer, Nicklaus, Player, Trevino, and Floyd. But it is gratifying beyond words for one of Crenshaw's age to have such reverence for golf's rich history, and the eloquence of its literature. (Now who's getting emotional?)

It was at this point, barely into my memory, that I realized I was selling short a marvelous golfing era. I had not even mentioned the triumphs and sometimes tribulations of Bobby

Locke, Peter Thomson, Arnold Palmer, Gary Player, Lee Trevino, Tom Watson, or Seve Ballesteros — to name but a precious few.

So I tore up the fledgling piece, telephoned the editor and told him I would have to change the terms of reference to at least double the number of magic moments to be described. He replied that he was publishing a magazine, not a bloody book, which is why this piece appears here.

In 1987 at Muirfield, Scotland, during the Open Championship, my wife and I had the good fortune to stay at the Open Arms, a magnificent "pub" in the charming village of Dirleton between Gullane and North Berwick. And I was amazed when, on going down for breakfast on the Saturday morning of the championship, with rain lashing down in buckets, borne on a bitterly cold 30-miles-per-hour wind from Siberia via the North Sea, I found four captains of American industry switching their clubs from their tournament bags to the Sunday variety in the lobby. As one of them asserted so correctly, "No caddy would be crazy enough to go out in this, but we've got an 11:30 starting time on Gullane Number One."

Having taken a brief foray to Muirfield that day, only to return to the hotel to watch third-round action on television, I later joined those four gentlemen in the bar. I was absolutely thrilled by their healthily flushed, weather-beaten faces and their obvious satisfaction at not only surviving their battle against the elements, but having thoroughly enjoyed it. And, to their proud credit, they had played a very tough and exposed golf course in a little over three hours. On that day they rediscovered part of the true spirit of golf.

The "Black Ball Box" is rumored to have been initiated at Muirfield, to help determine if this or that applicant was acceptable to The Royal Company of Edinburgh Golfers. The ominous nature of it cannot help but make one wonder if the rub-off of "the box" has helped create the scowl sometimes related to those who "serve" visitors to this magnificent golf course.

48. The 10th at Muirfield, *Scotland*

Several years ago while browsing a second-hand shop in Edinburgh, I came upon a marvelous tiny book by the famous Scottish-born golf course architect Dr. Alister Mackenzie entitled *Golf Architecture*. The book is particularly fascinating because it was published in 1920, years before Mackenzie designed three of his crowning glories — Augusta National, Cypress Point, and Royal Melbourne. In the book, Mackenzie selects what he considers to be the ideal golf holes of the day.

Firstly, he nominated the par-three eleventh at St. Andrews known as Eden — somewhat euphemistically — the dominating feature of whose 164 yards is the Strath bunker, the almost bottomless pit that threatens the front right-hand edge of the green, which is large and slopes severely down from back to front. The almost as notorious Hill bunker guards the left of the green.

Mackenzie also picked the eighth hole at Moortown, Leeds, England, known as Gibraltar. Members there might like to know that, in Mackenzie's words, "Its length is 170 yards, and it has been entirely artificially created at the small cost of 35 pounds sterling ($53)!"

Also from St. Andrews, Mackenzie nominated the sixteenth (Corner of the Dyke), then 338 yards long and now 380, as an ideal par four. Weather and wind conditions obviously determine how one is forced to play it, since it is dominated by the three bunkers known as the Principal's Nose in the middle of the fairway close to 250 yards from the tee. If these cannot be carried, the golfer must either flirt with the out-of-bounds fence all the way down the right-hand side or play to the left for safety, and then back toward the fence over Grant's and the Wig bunkers that menace the approach from this direction. One has lost count through the years of the great golfers who have driven into the Principal's Nose in moments of crisis, but certainly Arnold Palmer was one of them, in his first appearance in Scotland in the Centenary Open Championship of 1960.

49. Laurie's Shop, *St. Andrews, Scotland*

50. Walking the Dog at Turnberry, *on the firth of Clyde, Scotland*

Mackenzie rated the fourteenth or Long Hole of 560 yards at St. Andrews as "probably the best hole of its length in existence," because it could be played in so many different ways. Alas, the much-needed automatic watering system has since produced coarser grass that has long ago robbed the green, which tilts away from the player, of much of its fire. As Mackenzie said more than 70 years ago, the hole "is very nearly ideal, but would be better still if the lie of the land were such that the Beardies, the Crescent, the Kitchen and Hell bunkers were visible and impressive looking." It is indeed the hidden bunkers at St. Andrews that most world-class players complain about.

Mackenzie also nominated the par-four seventeenth hole — the Road Hole — at St. Andrews, now 460 yards long, as the last of the ideal holes, and who would argue with him about that one?

It is fascinating that no one knows who designed and constructed these great holes or whether they were just part of the natural terrain. But it is a fact that most renowned architects have copied one, if not all of them, somewhere in the world.

The classic modern-era example of never giving up was Billy Casper's victory in the 1966 U.S. Open, when he made up seven strokes on Arnold Palmer in the last nine holes at Olympic Club in San Francisco. Another example is Gary Player's triumph over the late Tony Lema at Wentworth, England, in the Piccadilly World match-play championship in 1965. The gutsy South African was seven holes down with 17 of his 36-hole match to play — and won on the 37th green.

But for me the most outrageous triumph against all odds occurred at Portland Golf Club, Oregon, on September 28, 1969, in the long-defunct Alcan "Golfer of the Year" championship. I shall never forget that Sunday afternoon for two reasons. Firstly, Casper made up seven strokes to beat Lee Trevino in the last three — yes,

three — holes. Secondly, that improbable comeback nearly ended my journalism career.

Time was running out as I ad-libbed my final-edition story by telephone off the television set in the pressroom to the *Financial Times* in London where, with a time differential of eight hours, it was already past midnight.

Under pressure from a jaded night editor anxious to put the newspaper — and himself — to bed, I felt safe enough to release my "intro" when I saw Trevino make a brilliant eagle three at the 511-yard, par-five fifteenth hole to extend his lead to six shots over Casper, who was playing immediately in front of him. My opening paragraph read, "Lee Trevino is coasting to victory here at Portland Golf Club in the Alcan 'Golfer of the Year' championship. With three holes to play he enjoys a comfortable six-strokes margin over his nearest rival, Billy Casper, who is cannily concentrating on second-place money of $15,000 to the winner's top-heavy share of $55,000 of the $139,000 purse."

I said good night to the night editor and strolled out to the seventeenth green just in time to realize that my opening paragraph was gibberish. It is still difficult to believe what actually happened in that momentous hour. Casper had birdied the last four holes from 20, eight, seven, and six feet, and was happy enough to have secured second place.

It appeared to matter little that Trevino had hooked his drive against a tree at the sixteenth hole and taken a bogey five. But when he and his caddie argued over the choice of club at the short seventeenth, Trevino chose to fly in the face of another golfing axiom that decrees "Only you must choose the club, since only you can hit the ball." Trevino allowed his own choice of an eight-iron to be overruled in favor of the nine proffered by his caddie.

Lee angrily rounded on his caddie as the ball plunged under the lip of the bunker short of the green into wet sand. At the second attempt to remove it, Trevino barely exploded the ball to the edge of the green. And as he sank his third putt for a triple-bogey six, Casper's fourth successive birdie was being heralded enthusiastically.

I fled the pressroom, told the *Financial Times* to kill my story, and watched flabbergasted as Trevino left himself an excellent chance to tie with a birdie putt from 15 feet. He missed, I dictated the correct result for the stop press, and prepared in a local hostelry for my inevitable dismissal. Thankfully the silence from London was golden.

Being a traditionalist, I have no use for the long putter currently in vogue. But I never voiced my opinion as clearly or cleverly as an Australian broadcaster with whom I shared the booth during the 1989 Palm Meadows Cup. I commented what an extraordinary thing it was that Aussie Peter Senior, once paralyzed by the yips, had won the Australian Open, the Australian PGA Championship and the lucrative Johnnie Walker Classic in little more than a month with his long putter anchored under his chin by his left hand. My cohort replied, "You're dead right, Ben, it is extraordinary, and all the more so because when he first held the thing he didn't know whether to suck it or blow it."

The PGA Tour once had on it an American Indian, Ky Lafoon. Bitterly angered after a terrible round someplace out west, he drove east for the next stop. As punishment to the cause of his anger, his driver, he tied the club to his automobile bumper.

My most embarrassing moment as a television announcer occurred in Chicago at the Western Open of 1976. In the early hours of Saturday morning as I paid a visit to the bathroom, I had a coughing fit and accidentally flushed my upper bridge down the john. The last glimpse I caught of my upper set was its final despairing spin before it dived into oblivion. I, too, made a despairing dive, but the suction was such that I was happy to retrieve my right arm, let alone the teeth.

A reluctant glance in the mirror revealed the full horror of the situation. Only my two big old buckled front teeth had survived an automobile racing accident 25 years previously. Talking without a lisp and whistle was out of the question.

I telephoned my ex-wife in England, but she became hysterical with callous mirth. I telephoned the hotel maintenance man, and he became considerably enraged at my suggestion that he should dredge for the precious dentures, and further appalled that, even if he were to find them, I should thereafter even think of wearing them. I telephoned CBS-TV's golf executive producer, Frank Chirkinian, and he, finding it hard to believe that I was either sober or serious, told me to meet him in the lobby in half an hour.

One look at my toothless grin convinced him that I would have to record my introductory description of the seventeenth hole tight lipped and at a different time from my fellow announcers. Frank knew only too well that the latter would do their evil worst to make me break up laughing. At this precise time cohort Jack Whitaker, or "Inspector Clouseau" as he is known for obvious reasons, appeared in the lobby in a state of disarray.

51. The Church Pews, *Oakmont, Pennsylvania. When Bobby Jones beat Watts Gunn for the U.S. Amateur in 1925, it was the first and only time two members of the same club had ever met in the finals. The U.S. Open has been played at Oakmont six times.*

52. Trap by the Windmill, *National Golf Links of America, Southampton, New York. It was here that Charles Blair Macdonald, the designer of the course, invited his son to opening day: When said son drove the first green and chided "Father" about the design . . . "Father" banished him from further play at the course!*

"What's wrong, Jack?" asked Chirkinian. "What's wrong?" replied Whitaker both loudly and angrily. "For the third time this season I've sent my slacks out for cleaning with the rental car keys in the pocket."

Chirkinian said quietly, with menace, "For once, Jack, you have done nothing nearly so stupid as this dumb Limey. Now show Jack your mouth." The lost keys were forgotten in the ensuing laughter.

Despite Chirkinian's assertions that I was crazy, I was determined to go in search of teeth. And sure enough, on reaching the CBS Sports complex at Butler National Golf Club, I was able to deprive an associate director of his 10:30 dentist appointment. I was quickly driven by a young man with local knowledge to the dentist's office, where all had been forewarned of my impending arrival.

"What appears to be the problem?" asked the charming young dentist. "The problem is — I've no . . . teeth," I replied, grinning. The dentist, duly horrified, sprang into furious action, canceling appointments and having his assistant quickly take impressions of my upper jaw. Four hours later the incredible dentist delivered a new set of teeth which only fitted perfectly. My career had been saved.

But the CBS technicians were not about to let the incident go unnoticed. That evilly ingenious bunch had scoured the neighborhood in the morning and found a mouthful — both upper and lower sets — of wind-up, mechanical teeth. That afternoon in our rehearsal shortly before going on the air, I looked for my face to come up in the announcers' sequence on my monitor screen and listened for the usual parrotlike delivery, "I'm Ben Wright, and I'll be reporting the play from the 456-yard seventeenth hole . . ." and so on, but there was no me. Instead, the aforesaid villainous scoundrels had positioned the mechanical clack-

ers alongside the flagstick on the seventeenth green, and it was the teeth which were doing the talking for me, perfectly synchronized to my delivery.

In 1966, on the day of the greatest April blizzard in England for 80 years, the public schools old boys' foursomes teams set out to contest the first round of their annual Halford Hewitt knockout tournament at Deal and Royal St. George's. At mid-afternoon, with the snow being driven horizontally by a force-nine gale, play had to be abandoned on both courses. But not before several competitors had risked serious harm or death.

This is no exaggeration. Some of these gentlemen had to be helped into the respective clubhouses and revived. One of the eldest could not even remember having played golf, or being expected to try, in such appalling conditions.

The wise ones were those who conceded their matches after one token drive, or after taking too many shots at the first hole.

53. Working Together

Unfortunately for this correspondent, who eventually reached a dangerous state of mind in which he didn't care whether he lived or died, no one in my group suggested running for cover until we were finally ordered in from Royal St. George's remote ninth green. By that time many stiff upper lips were frozen rigid, and running was out of the question. But to be ordered to resume hostilities at the tenth tee at breakfast time on the following morning was perhaps the unkindest cut of all.

Like most others, I wore pyjamas underneath almost every other article I had packed. An overcoat, worn between shots, became so heavy with snow that it was almost impossible to lift with numbed hands. Three golf gloves had been soaked before the fourth green was reached. Fur-lined leather gloves were ruined — and hands stained brown. In fact, from neck to waist I finished a vivid red with the dye from my roll-neck cotton sweater, bright green from waist down by my pyjamas. The water squirted up each trouser leg with every step to induce a rapid paralysis of the knees.

One of my opponents was forced eventually to take off his spectacles, and he wandered around almost helpless thereafter in a myopic nightmare world of his own.

The flight of the ball was well nigh impossible to follow, since by lifting the head one was guaranteed several sharp smacks in the eyeballs from snowflakes or hailstones.

The zips on my golf bag were clogged with frozen snow when I hurled it into the boot of my car that evening, and they had not melted the following morning.

I shall never forget the remark made by my one of my teammates as I helped him on with his sodden trench coat in the hut by the eighth hole. Asked how his match stood, he replied angrily, "We were four down, but like stupid bastards we've won two back."

I must confess that the utter misery of it all brought out the worst in me. As my teammate's beautiful, hand-knitted sweater lengthened visibly under its weight of snow as we waited to hit, I couldn't resist advising him not to play a full shot, in case the garment slipped off his shoulders and grabbed him in a half nelson. His tee shot duly flew high and left onto a sandhill — and his club flew almost as high and at least half as far.

I had my comeuppance at the ninth, however. There I claimed to have hit my partner's brand-new ball down the middle of the fairway. But by then the snow that had swept horizontally over the district without landing since dawn was finally settling. We didn't find that ball until the following morning, by which time we had conceded the hole — and it was in the rough.

The hero of the tournament for me was a local brewer who appeared purple-faced out of the blizzard on the ninth fairway to dispense brandy. When offered a swig, my teammate nobly pointed out that there was very little left in the proffered bottle, to which the brewer replied somewhat tipsily that there were two full ones somewhere inside the mountain of clothing he was wearing.

On the previous Sunday I had written in *The Sunday Times* about a football match at Burnley played in torrential rain in six inches of mud, saying that "on occasions like these one begins to doubt the sanity of one's countrymen." Now I'm certain.

54. The Stout Drinker

55. The Maintenance Shack, *Nairn, Scotland*

56. The Awesome 17th at Kiawah, *Kiawah Island, South Carolina, site of the USA's inspirational Ryder Cup Victory in 1991*

The biennial Ryder Cup matches, in which the once perennial American winners face Europe's best professionals in genuine match play, attracted about as much attention among casual golfers in the States as the America's Cup contest stirred the hearts of those who mess about in sport boats — that is, until the Americans finally lost both trophies. Suddenly the Ryder Cup matches appear to have all the magical ingredients and heart-warming appeal of the game's much debated and elusive "fifth major."

Even so, many Americans remain blissfully ignorant of the true nature of the contest. For instance, at the 1987 match played at the Muirfield Village Golf Club in Dublin, Ohio, I arrived at the eighteenth green in late morning on the first day's play and, to my astonishment, found it encircled by several hundred local spectators.

"What are you waiting around here for?" I asked one of the throng.

"For the first match to arrive any time now," was his reply.

I tried to explain that this was real match play with no guarantee that any of the four matches would last as far as the eighteenth hole. Yet many of those fans, conditioned by years of dreadful "made for television" events, remained firm. Only one of the matches that day reached the eighteenth green, but for that one, the steadfast crowd had an excellent view.

One cringes to think that these glorious sporting events, filled with so much strategy, psychology, and emotion, and now deservingly admired, once almost faced extinction for lack of interest. It was indeed difficult to muster much interest from 1957 through 1985, as the Americans won 14 consecutive Ryder Cups. Largely in the hope of giving the British and Irish a better chance of victory, and at the same time perhaps attracting even minimal spectator and television interest in America, the format of the matches was changed no fewer than five times — in 1961, 1963, 1977, and twice in 1979. The second of the '79 changes — which joined European players with the British and Irish — probably saved the Ryder Cup.

My earliest memory of the matches goes back to 1953, when Henry Cotton and Lloyd Mangrum were the respective captains at Wentworth, Surrey, England. In a pulsatingly close finish, victory for the home side finally rested in the hands of two desperately young and inexperienced Englishmen, Peter Alliss and Bernard Hunt.

But unfortunately Alliss snatched defeat from the jaws of victory, losing at the last hole to Joe Turnesa, while Hunt only halved his match against Dave Douglas. Both had looked likely to win, and were expected to do so by a huge crowd starved of victory for far too long. Hunt and Alliss were both pilloried by the British press, most viciously by the dreaded tabloids, and I firmly believe were never the same again in a playing sense, never winning a major championship between them. America won by 6 1/2 points to 5 1/2.

The Ryder Cup

The Ryder Cup atmosphere became electric only at Lindrick in 1957 when the British and Irish captain, the remarkably competitive Dai Rees, had a furious verbal battle with one of his team members, heavyweight, Shropshire-born Harry Weetman. After their much publicized feud, Rees dropped Weetman from the singles, and his team rallied round him. But I believe the pattern was set for a momentous second day when Tommy Bolt walked onto the first tee and said to his opponent, the fiery Scot Eric Brown, "You're beat, sucker." Brown was sufficiently incensed to become fired up in the best possible way, and with Peter Mills beating American captain Jackie Burke even more easily than Brown crushed

57. *Pinehurst #2, Pinehurst, North Carolina*

Bolt, those playing behind the pair became inspired and clinched a rare victory.

Nothing much went right for the British and Irish until the 1969 match, which closely followed Tony Jacklin's epic British Open triumph just north on the Lancashire coastline at Royal Lytham. Not surprisingly, the home team was fired up at Royal Birkdale. There was even an unseemly shouting match between Welshman Brian Huggett and his uncompromising Scottish partner Bernard Gallacher and their American opponents Dave Hill and Ken Still, the four walking down the eighth fairway on the second afternoon in their four-ball match literally yelling insults at each other.

Eventually the outcome of the match depended on the last two singles matches still on the course in the gathering gloom. Jacklin had beaten Jack Nicklaus by 4 and 3 in the final single of the morning. When Huggett halved his single with Billy Casper in late afternoon, he collapsed in tears in the arms of Eric Brown, his captain, in the mistaken belief that his half point had won the match for his team. In fact, it all came down to the very last match, in which Jacklin and Nicklaus were locked in mortal combat for the second time that fateful day. Jacklin was finally left with a putt of some three feet to halve both his match and the entire series against his great rival.

And then Nicklaus performed the singular most sporting act I have ever seen perpetrated on any field of sport, let alone the golf course. He calmly picked up Jacklin's ball, making sure that the match and series were both halved. As Nicklaus said so generously afterward, he did not think that such an epic three-day struggle should have to depend on a single putt of that tantalizing length.

To this day I am confident that Jacklin, at best a very ordinary putter from such distances, would have missed that putt, so great was the pressure upon his shoulders, exerted as it was by an entire nation too long committed to witnessing, and suffering, agonizing defeat.

Nicklaus's behavior was also, for me, the most memorable aspect of the 1973 Ryder Cup at Muirfield. Drawn against England's Clive Clark and Ulsterman Eddie Polland in the second afternoon four-ball, Nicklaus and teammate Tom Weiskopf were overwhelming favorites. Barbara Nicklaus, eight months pregnant, had walked 18 holes to support the pair during the morning, but on the first tee of the afternoon match she told her husband she might not go all the way. Jack replied loudly, "It won't be a long walk," a remark certainly overheard by the Brits.

On the first green, Weiskopf's ball was within 10 feet of the hole in two, while Nicklaus's ball was twice as far away. As Nicklaus walked past his partner, he hissed, "Pick your ball up, Tom."

"What the hell are you talking about?" replied Weiskopf.

"I said, pick up your ball."

A bewildered Weiskopf told me years later that he complied, whereupon Nicklaus calmly rammed in his putt. Clark and Polland did well to lose by only 3 and 2.

The 1987 match at Muirfield Village had finally attracted major network television coverage, and the event proved worthy with the quality of its golf and the level of its drama. At Muirfield Village in Dublin, Ohio, the European team achieved its first victory ever on American soil. That alone was highly dramatic,

The legendary "Putter Boy" at Pinehurst

but emotions rose to the level of melodrama since the American team was captained by Jack Nicklaus, proud designer of the Muirfield Village course.

Apart from the stellar quality of the golf produced on that occasion, there was a touching camaraderie between the thousands of supporters of each side, waving as they did with much gusto their miniature flags, the Union Jack and the Stars and Stripes. The latter made a rather tardy appearance, however, becoming ubiquitous only after Nicklaus publicly appealed for more support for his beleaguered squad. I believe that many lasting international friendships were forged that weekend to obliterate from memory the questionable-at-best behavior of the British fans at The Belfry in 1985 when Europe won for the first time since the British and Irish accomplished that feat at Lindrick, Nottinghamshire, England, 28 years previously in 1957.

The 1989 Ryder Cup match played at The Belfry and its historic 14-14 tie has to be elevated above even the Muirfield Village triumph, in my humble estimation. To my mind it was the perfect sporting occasion.

In Africa some of the native tribes have a custom of beating the ground with clubs and uttering spine chilling cries. Anthropologists call this a form of self expression. In America, we call it Golf.

How different it might have been had the Americans been able to play the eighteenth hole, a strong, right-angle dogleg to the left, par four, with carries over a lake required by both drive and second shot. On the final day, with the match in the balance, Americans Paul Azinger, Payne Stewart, and Mark Calcavecchia all hit their drives on the eighteenth into the lake, and Calcavecchia compounded the felony by hitting his third shot into the lake as well.

Long-hitting Fred Couples was bitten by another sort of demon on the pivotal eighteenth — the pressure of the Ryder Cup. His opponent for the match, journeyman Christy O'Connor, Jr., had driven short and was left with a difficult two-iron to the green. He struck a masterful shot, however, that pulled up only four feet from the hole. Couples, who had only a nine-iron to the flag, was so unnerved that he missed the green and took a woeful bogey five to lose.

Curtis Strange won each of the last four holes of his match against Ian Woosnam with birdies to level the score at 14-14 and provided a finish worthy of an unforgettable happening.

Golf was the big winner again in the 1991 Ryder Cup matches played at beautiful Kiawah Island, although there are those who opine that Pete Dye's diabolical Ocean Course bloodied and battered both teams with equal ferocity. For the series to have depended on the final putt of the last singles match was so extraordinarily dramatic that any Hollywood film scriptwriter presenting such a scenario would have been told quickly by any self-respecting agent that such a plot was too far-fetched.

Having said that, however, I must quarrel with the conditioning of a course that allows it to make fools of the best golfers in the world. I do not enjoy, nor do I believe that fans of golf enjoy, watching the golfers whose marvelous skills I so admire and envy winning holes in bogey or even double bogey. In the immortal words of broadcaster Steve Melnyk, "Par should be a meaningful score."

I am only grateful to have been present to witness a historic, epic and well-deserved American victory. It was a display worthy of the great sporting tradition that the Ryder Cup has become.

58. Spring Foursome, *The Greenbrier, West Virginia*

59. The 17th at Medinah, *Chicag*

I well remember my first meeting with Pete Dye, that eccentric and erratic golf architectural genius, in the early 1970s. Dye had just returned from Scotland after one of many trips he made across the Atlantic with his wife Alice, one of the foremost women golfers in America then and now. Dye waxed lyrical that day on the subject of the great Scottish links layouts and how American designers needed to get back to basics and build more natural, less manicured courses in the time-honored British and Irish tradition. It was an admirable idea, but something went sadly awry in its achievement.

The inventive and much-imitated Pete proceeded to usher in an era of design that he, and most of his rival architects, designated as their "neo-Scottish" period. A far more accurate designation might have been "pseudo-Scottish." Deep grass bunkers, pot bunkers, humps and hollows, and absurd chocolate-drop mounds, all with impossibly steep slopes, so-called "waste" bunkers for their hard, unkempt, and very large surface areas of sand or soil dotted with sundry unruly and scrofulous growths of native vegetation, but most of all a profusion of railroad ties used by the thousands to shore up everything — tees, bunkers, and sometimes huge man-made lakes and ponds. Dye, and to a lesser extent his imitators, went to such extremes that jokes were cracked about his having single-handedly put the American railroad systems out of business. And I believe it was Sam Snead who first joked that Dye had created the only golf courses in the world that could actually burn down!

A bizarre sort of competition soon began, apparently to determine who among these architects could rearrange the most cubic tons of earth to create the most demonic course. By doing so, such courses became monuments to their builders rather than venues for recreation and sport. The elderly, who usually constitute the majority of those financially able to live on or near such facilities, quickly tire of playing these monsters, being physically inadequate for the task. Even younger participants grow weary of such relentless challenge. Golf, after all, was never intended to be labor.

Thankfully there are many American, British, and European architects whose philosophy has always been to create courses for the maximum enjoyment of the majority of golfers. Even Dye has done excellent work that does not fall into the plastic and largely unplayable category to which I refer, such as the magnificent Harbour Town Links on Hilton Head Island, perhaps the outstanding flatland classic of the modern era. And there is no doubt in my mind that The Golf Club in New Albany, Ohio, is Dye's (and the game's) most brilliant hidden gem, so jealously do the members guard their privacy. Jack Nicklaus, who like Dye can be prone to occasional design excess, created one of the best modern designs at Shoal Creek in Birmingham, Alabama.

It seems to me that American designers should forget forever their obsession with Scottish, Irish, Welsh, or English courses and restart doing what two Scotsmen accomplished so admirably in the United States and elsewhere in the earlier years of this century. The prolific Scot, Donald Ross, and his urbane countryman, Dr. Alister Mackenzie, largely adapted their designs to the beautiful contours of the prime land they inherited, and, in the absence of major earth-moving machinery, what followed was probably the golden age of American golf course architecture. Recently *Golf* magazine asked a panel of 64 experts to select the top 25 courses in the world, and only one of those cited — Muirfield Village in Dublin, Ohio — was built after World War II.

Some masterpieces of golf architecture were based on traditional values. Charles Blair Macdonald (Chicago Golf Club, National Links, Mid Ocean Club in Bermuda, to name but three of his masterpieces); Walter Travis (both courses at Westchester Country Club, the redesign of Garden City, the original nine at Sea Island, Georgia); Henry C. Fownes and his son William (Oakmont); George C. Thomas (Los Angeles North and South, Riviera and Bel-Air); Albert W. Tillinghast (Baltusrol Upper and Lower and Ridgewood in

60. Pebble Beach, *California, 18th hole*

New Jersey, Winged Foot East and West, Five Farms in Baltimore, San Francisco Golf Club, and one of my personal favorites, Brook Hollow, almost in downtown Dallas); Hugh Wilson (both courses at Merion Cricket Club); William S. Glynn and Howard C. Toomey (Spring Mill in Philadelphia, the Cascades course at The Homestead in Virginia, Cherry Hills in Denver); George A. Crump (Pine Valley); and Jack Neville and Douglas Grant (Pebble Beach) were some of the most brilliantly successful, many of them amateurs whose best designs were their first and only.

Several of these Americans studied Scottish courses, but the best lesson they learned was that the finest courses in that country, the cradle of golf, followed the existing contours of the terrain. Their greens were never too large nor too severely contoured. Have you realized how difficult a straight putt on a predominantly flat surface can be? Mackenzie's Augusta National greens have become too severe for some competitors only at recent Masters tournaments because the club chose to switch to the much finer, and in my opinion superior, bent grass from the old mixture of Bermuda overseeded with rye in the winter.

But there are many recent trends in American design that are admirable and should be encouraged worldwide. For example, the subtle use of multiple tees, at least four per hole, encourages women, juniors, and the elderly without detriment to superior players. The replacement of sand bunkers, many acres of them purely cosmetic, by grass bunkers is praiseworthy, as is placing sand only on the flat base of bunkers rather than all the way up deeply etched faces. Two and even three tiers on a green, which permits more varied pin placements, is much preferable to the

ridiculously severe undulations that make putting a nightmare for all but the world's best professionals. Practice facilities are becoming larger and more comprehensive, as the game's incredible current boom demands.

American golf architects, in my opinion, are better innovators than imitators.

61. The 5th at Pine Valley, *Clementon, New Jersey*

As a betting man, one of the more fortunate experiences of my life was to venture out in a miserable drizzle to take a first admiring look at Merion on the eve of the 1971 U.S. Open. By pure chance I picked up Lee Trevino on the first hole. The next three hours or so were as fascinating as any I ever spent, as Trevino nominated each shot he was to produce and duly shaped it to achieve his aim to finish below the hole every time. It was a virtuoso performance that had me hustling to my typewriter and later to phone my bookmaker in London.

My money was far from easily won, however, and I still regard the 18-hole playoff for the title between Trevino and Nicklaus, after the two had tied at level par, as the best possible vindication of the choice of a venue little over 6,500 yards in length.

Just over a year later at Muirfield, Scotland, on Trevino's 71st hole of the 1972 Open Championship, I saw him lose control of his emotions for the first time. Trevino had started his backswing on the tee when the well-known shout of "Fore!" was roared out by a gallery marshal a few yards away. A cameraman had ventured into the fairway some 250 yards away and promptly scuttled back into the crowd. But Trevino was forced to back off twice, on the second occasion by the cameraman's assistant. He never became comfortable when he resumed his stance, and his drive skittered away into the fairway bunker on the left. Lee hurried to the ball muttering again and again, "That damned photographer has cost me my title."

He took no care whatsoever over his second shot, the ball squirting into the right-hand rough, or on the third, which landed on a high bank behind the green. Even as he hit the fourth shot, he was boiling. Trevino told me later he had only these two cameramen on his mind when he whipped out his nine-iron and chipped the ball straight into the hole on the 542-yard par five.

Tony Jacklin, level with Trevino going to that fateful seventeenth tee, was 16 feet from the hole in three shots. He had watched helplessly the previous day as Trevino had thinned his bunker shot across the sixteenth green hard against the flagstick and into the hole. Now he again watched his opponent chip in from behind the seventeenth green, and Jacklin fell apart. It is so easy to be wise after the event, but Jacklin was never the same. He three-putted 17, made bogey from the right-hand bunker at the last and lost second place to Nicklaus's 66.

Many thought Nicklaus, who had already won The Masters and U.S. Open that year, was too defensive for too long at Muirfield, and it cost him his Grand Slam bid. Bob Drum, the journalist who "invented Arnold Palmer," was the only one who would dare to rip into Nicklaus to that effect. And he did so at the most hilarious Open Championship party I have ever attended.

It was the next year, and Tom Weiskopf had just enjoyed his finest hour, winning the 1973 British Open at Troon. He had invited several of us for dinner at the Marine Hotel adjacent to the eighteenth fairway. Long into the night, Drum suddenly turned on Nicklaus and said in his gravelly voice, "You're a damn coward. You know why you lost last year? You know why you only finished fourth here? Because you pussyfoot around with a three-wood and a one-iron when you're the finest driver of the ball in the world. Just take your driver, your wedge and putt as well as you always do and you'll win everything." Within a month

> Leave it to Lee Trevino to come up with a classic comment about Merion: "I'm in love with Merion and I don't even know her last name!"

Nicklaus had won the PGA Championship at Canterbury, Ohio.

Later that night a Scottish baritone in full Highland dress, kilt and all, sang a eulogy, extolling the golfing talents of Weiskopf and Nicklaus as the pair shuffled their feet more than a little embarrassedly. They simply had to reply to such a tribute, so the two locked arms and broke into a rendition of "Amazing Grace," sounding very much like a tune one might have expected from a set of out-of-tune bagpipes.

Our flight from London's Heathrow Airport to Adelaide, South Australia, with a change of airline in Sydney, took off three hours late, and became ever later at every stop along the way. But it still came as a profound and hideous surprise when I emerged bleary-eyed from customs and immigration and the baggage claim area to be told by an attractive lady courtesy car driver that, "We'd better get the hell out of here quick. You're on the air for four hours starting at two o'clock, which gives us just under an hour. . . ."

The drive to the Grange Golf Club and the first round of the 1978 West Lakes Classic that fateful Thursday afternoon remains a blur in my memory. But as a former race driver, I could not in any way, shape or form criticize the inspired performance of my driver — masterly rapid.

I quickly said "Good-bye" to my hosts on arrival at the club, and excused myself for a quick trip to the Press Room. It seemed like a good idea to find out who was playing in the tournament. A quick glance at the scoreboard gave me the names of the players co-commentator Graham "Swampy" Marsh

and myself were likely to be watching over the next four long hours, and there was just one real mystery man among them. I knew that the N. in N. Suzuki stood for Norio, because I had seen him play previously. But I had no idea what the Y. in Y. Suzuki represented.

Alas, only one intrepid Australian reporter was busily typing in the Press Room during this, the hour when a free lunch was available, and I rudely interrupted his honest toil to ask him if he could enlighten me about the first name of Y. Suzuki.

Yeah, mate," he replied without either looking up or stopping his urgent typing. "It's Yastartyamota."

"Pardon me," I said. "Could you please spell that out for me?"

"No worries, mate," this gnarled gnome replied, again without

62. Basket Flag at Merion, *Ardmore, Pennsylvania. The Baskets atop the flag sticks were born of a pilgrimage made by Hugh Wilson, a Merion member who was asked to design a new course. He went to England where he could study the architecture of British courses. He saw the wicker basket–topped flag sticks at Sunningdale, near London, and decided they belonged at Merion too. They were woven by the then greenskeeper and his staff who had learned basket weaving in their native Italy. Way before Sunningdale, these baskets were used by shepherds who protected their lunches in them while playing golf.*

looking up or breaking stride on his ancient machine. "It's YASTARTYAMOTA Suzuki."

I thanked my informant, and within minutes we were on the air. And as luck would have it, we were barely half an hour into the broadcast when Y. Suzuki came into camera range. To my eternal discredit, I referred to the Japanese player as Youstartyourmotor Suzuki, and Marsh's face had to be seen to be believed as he almost fell backward out of the tower in a quite hysterical fit of mirthful glee.

Marsh thought I was joking, but I was merely bewildered, and still the penny failed to drop. Every time thereafter the aforementioned Mr. Suzuki came onto the screen, I greeted him by his five-syllable first name — to Marsh's palpable amazement. People who tell me they are not really affected by jet lag don't tend to capture my attention.

Opinion will forever be fiercely divided on the fascinating subject of what exactly constitutes a perfect golf course or even a perfect hole — if either exists.

There is such a world of difference between the rugged oceanic terrain of the glorious Monterey Peninsula in California and the rolling, flowering, shrub-covered hills of Augusta National Golf Club, or the bleak, treeless expanses of most British seaside links, that comparisons are often invidious. Yet Cypress Point and Pebble Beach, Augusta, and Muirfield, Scotland, are all perfect examples of their type, in my mind. And so is Pine Valley, built early in this century in rural Clementon, New Jersey, by George Crump, a Philadelphia hotelier and amateur architect — one of a talented breed. Pine Valley is perhaps the roughest and most punishing inland course in the world.

But if I had to nominate 10, and no more than 10, courses on which to play for the rest of my life, they would be, in approximately alphabetical order: Augusta National, Cypress Point, Merion (East), Muirfield (Scotland), Pine Valley, Shinnecock Hills, Sunningdale's Old Course (England), Turnberry's Ailsa (Scotland), Woodhall Spa (in remote Lincolnshire, England), and one from the Antipodes, Royal Melbourne composite (Australia).

The average golfer probably recognizes most of these, but I have yet to meet an American who has even heard of Woodhall Spa. Those who have tried it on my recommendation have been unanimously lavish in their praise. It is surely one of the golf world's hidden gems. Woodhall Spa is literally an oasis in the virtually treeless Lincolnshire fen country, roughly 200 miles north of London. The fen country consists of mile upon mile of very flat and exceedingly fertile agricultural land with dark, almost muddy soil.

As for Royal Melbourne, the composite course (which is regularly used for tournament play) is made up of the best 18 of 36 wonderful holes set on this city's golf-rich sandbar, which can boast at least 10 other layouts in the top class. Its appeal lies largely in its surprising and beguiling mix of trees and heather-strewn heathland and bleak linksland. Its greens may be the best and fastest in the world. This arguably could be Mackenzie's finest creation.

What constitutes a perfect golf hole? It certainly doesn't have to be immensely long. The 107-yard, par-three seventh hole at Pebble Beach and the 126-yard "Postage Stamp" eighth at Troon in Scotland are photographed as often as any in the world, and rightly so. They are equally fascinating because what demands a wedge or nine-iron in calm conditions can become as much as a two- or three-iron — or even a wooden club shot — when the wind and surf hammer in off

63. A Testing 3 at Royal Birkdale, *Southport, England*

the Pacific Ocean or the Firth of Clyde, respectively.

The most photographed hole of all is, without doubt, the 233-yard sixteenth at Cypress Point, designed by the legendary Mackenzie. Played from cliff top to cliff top above the boiling surf, usually into the teeth of the wind blowing off the ocean, this is always a heroic hole even for champions. But for the mere hacker there is the safer route by land down the promontory to the left. A modest tee shot to this area can set up a short iron pitch to the green and occasionally even yield the most pleasing of pars. In any case, even a bogey four on this gem is mightily satisfying to most club golfers.

Many of the best holes offer alternatives attractive to the expert and duffer alike, not to speak of their scenic beauty. This is why the short inward par fives at Augusta, the 465-yard thirteenth with its tributary of Rae's Creek menacing every inch of its length, and the 500-yard fifteenth with the ponds in front and beyond its shallow green, perennially provide high drama at the Masters tournament. Who will ever forget Nicklaus's eagle three at the fifteenth that helped him to win his twentieth major title at Augusta in 1986, or Seve Ballesteros's four-iron shot that plunged into the pond some half hour later to deprive the swashbuckling Spaniard of his coveted third green coat?

In short, it does not require dramatic undulations or even brilliant natural scenery to produce the best courses or the best holes. It does require the best architects, however.

Play had been rained out on a miserable, wickedly violent, stormy day at the 1988 British Open at Royal Lytham and St. Anne's. Even such a fast and efficiently draining links was virtually under water. Tables at any self-respecting restaurant in this once fashionable holiday resort, now a drab succession of mean streets full of little Victorian red brick houses mostly joined at the hip as if huddling together for warmth, were at a premium that night. Thankfully my wife discovered a charming, if raucous, little Italian family restaurant. After an interminable wait and more than one cocktail, we were ushered through the tightly packed room to a table for two alongside one for six, at which were seated a collection of obviously well-to-do, well-fed, and definitely overtrained Englishmen, who were passing a bottle of fine cognac between them as they rowdily struck some particularly large bets on the eventual outcome of the event.

Plainly intrigued by my wife's American accent, one of these noisy gentlemen pulled his seat over and engaged her in earnest conversation. When she told him that I was over from America to write about the championship, but that my primary job was with CBS television, announcing American golf tournaments, the unknown, rather tipsy visitor became quite animated and very opinionated. Apparently he was in the habit of watching every American tournament broadcast put out by the British television networks. Soon the stranger and my wife were discussing personalities and pondering what had become of various commentators he had listened to through the years.

64. Clubhouse at Medina, *Chicago*

All this time I was an interested if frustrated listener. But my eyes burst out like organ stops when our chatty friend suddenly blurted out, "And whatever happened to old Ben Wright?"

At last I had a chance to get a word in edgeways. "I am he," I roared, poking myself in the chest with my right index finger.

"No, you're not," our man replied. "I'm talking about *old* Ben Wright. I listened to that elderly guy years and years ago. He sounded like a retired schoolmaster and he must be long dead by now."

Vainly did my wife and myself strive to convince him that I had been writing

65. The Approach at Shinnecock Hills, *Southampton, New York*

about and broadcasting golf for some 34 years. Finally I even had to produce my British passport and North Carolina driver's license, and even then our man was only halfway convinced. He immediately left his friends and the restaurant furiously nodding his head, probably still in disbelief, and I never saw him again. But his curse lingers on at home. To my dear wife Kitty and my daughter Margaret, I shall be forever known as "Old Ben Wright."

One of the more regrettable aspects of the aging process is a tendency to look back frequently and fondly at the "good old days," a retrospective longing which understandably infuriates the young and comparatively inexperienced. Yet any journalist fortunate enough to have been courted by the Masters golf tournament in the late 1960s surely would recall the experience with glee.

On joining *The Financial Times* of London as that august newspaper's first golf correspondent in 1966, I immediately became the beneficiary of then Masters tournament chairman Mr. Clifford Roberts' policy of attracting — at any cost — the foreign press to ensure the event's stature as the newest of the four major championships. Roberts, regarded by the majority of those who came into close contact with him as an iron-fisted tyrant, wisely realized, as had the then ailing Mr. Bobby Jones, his cofounder at the Augusta National, that to woo the world's better class of golf writers was the perfect way to maximize the tournament's exposure.

Mr. Jack Stephens, the Masters tournament's latest in a short line of chairmen, told me a few years ago that Mr. Roberts had singled him out in the early sixties as the man who was entirely to orchestrate the planned invasion of invited British and Irish writers. Happily my name was added to that list in 1968. And what an experience that first trip to America and Augusta turned out to be!

My colleagues and I were flown first-class from London Heathrow to Kennedy and then promptly whisked by limousine to the Butler Aviation terminal at LaGuardia, where we boarded the aircraft provided by Mr. Stephens — anonymously, I must add — suitably loaded with cocktails and cordials. Duly refreshed and fortified, we were red carpeted into the charming Augusta airport, which has retained much of that charm to this day. Our baggage was loaded into one of the club's black limousines. The late Henry Longhurst, Leonard Crawley, Pat Ward-Thomas, and this still surviving new recruit to the good life were loaded into another bound for Augusta National and that first mesmeric ride down incomparable Magnolia Lane to the simple clubhouse.

In due course we were handed the keys to our spanking new Augusta National automobiles replete with the club's logo on the doors, into which our respective baggage had already been thoughtfully loaded. We drove in convoy behind our guide — on the wrong side of the road for my first time — to the palatial mansion complete with swimming pool that our benefactor had thoughtfully provided. Mr. Stephens, again anonymously, had even brought his own delightful retainers from Little Rock, Arkansas, to cater to our every whim. Needless to say, the tournament was fully and lovingly reported by our entire crew.

I was not to meet our benefactor for many years after that, eventually being introduced to Mr. Stephens by my CBS colleague Pat Summerall. Summerall had likewise been a beneficiary of Mr. Stephens' generosity many years previously when he had arrived on a football scholarship at the University of Arkansas without an overcoat to his name. Mr. Stephens quickly put right that oversight by providing a magnificent one for the newly arrived fledgling Florida football star.

Is there any wonder that I look back on my first Augusta National experience as "the good old days"? I'll risk the barbs of my younger colleagues.

66. TPC Sawgrass, *Ponte Vedra, Florida*

My first golf-related job as a cub reporter for the *Daily Dispatch* newspaper in Manchester, England, in 1954 was to "ghost" a weekly column for the late, great Scottish professional George Duncan. After we had decided on our subject for the week, and before I returned to my lodgings to write the piece, Duncan would play a nine-hole game with me at Mere Golf and Country Club, Cheshire, at which he reigned as professional for the club's first 27 years. It was a daunting experience which seldom took longer than one hour to complete. Not for nothing did George entitle his book *Golf at the Gallop*.

He would walk up behind his golf ball with his head canted to the right as he summed up the problems involved and his idea of their solution, select a club and hit it, hardly breaking stride. On the greens he would give each putt almost a cursory look before striking it. Consequently I was always breathing hard, struggling to keep up. But it was a refreshing and rewarding experience to be privileged to play alongside one of the greatest of all Scottish golfers, albeit usually on the receiving end, and although Duncan was in his seventies at the time. His mind worked every bit as quickly as did his aging body.

When George died on January 15, 1964, he was the last surviving Scottish-born winner of the British Open domiciled in Great Britain. He had won the Open in 1920 after two rounds of 80 at Royal Cinque Ports Golf Club in Deal, Kent, which left him 13 strokes behind the leader, his best friend Abe Mitchell. Duncan finished with rounds of 71 and 72 to win by two shots from Sandy Herd, with Mitchell two shots further back in fourth place, one behind Ted Ray.

Two years later in 1922, Duncan finished second to Walter Hagen in a palpitating finish at nearby Royal St. George's, Kent. Hagen had finished the course and was being hailed as the winner when the news filtered through from the course that Duncan, a very late starter, was burning up the course and required a four at the last hole to tie with a phenomenal round of 68. Alas, George took five for 69 in an age when sub-70 scores were very rare.

Prior to the First World War, Duncan was a frequent challenger to the great triumvirate of Harry Vardon, James Braid, and J. H. Taylor, and he would certainly have achieved even greater fame had not the war intervened when he was in his prime.

Every time I witness the slow play which so plagues the game of golf today, I think fondly of this dear friend.

At Pebble Beach in January 1986, I asked Greg Norman to compete in a skins game the following September at my club, Kenmure, in rural Flat Rock, North Carolina, to benefit the Pardee Hospital in nearby Hendersonville, and Greg accepted. He and Chip Beck, runner-up to Ray Floyd in June that year in the U.S. Open at Shinnecock Hills, and the eminent seniors Miller Barber and Gene Littler were to compete for $1,000 per hole in better-ball team play — juniors against seniors. So, if Norman and Beck won all 18 holes, they would pocket but $9,000 each, and I could guarantee all four players no more than $3,000 each as a minimum. Chicken feed, indeed.

What a summer it was for Norman! He led all four majors going into the final round, although he won only one, the British Open at Turnberry. But Norman also won the European Open, and the World Matchplay Championship, and he led the Australian team to victory in the Dunhill Cup, three triumphs that came within a month. My friends in North Carolina were elated at our good fortune.

But when play was rained out during the third round of the European Open on Saturday, September 13, at Sunningdale — two days before Greg was due in Flat Rock — my small world crumbled. Norman had played only two holes when the third round was aborted. He was told he would have to play 34 more the following day, with a start soon after dawn. It seemed extremely unlikely that he would be able to catch the Concorde that Sunday night at 7 p.m., as we had planned. And so it turned out, because Norman was taken to the second hole of sudden death before he accounted for Scotland's Ken Brown.

I shall never forget our subsequent trans-Atlantic telephone conversation.

"Do you still want me to try to get there?" asked Greg.

"Do I still want you? If you don't show, you'll never see me again. They'll hang me from the tallest tree," I agonized.

"OK, mate. I'll be on the morning Concorde, if you can pick me up in New York," said Norman.

I duly had a chartered jet waiting and warmed up, Norman was whisked to Asheville, and a police officer gave our courtesy car a high-speed escort with blue lights flashing to Kenmure.

To my astonishment, British Airways had misplaced Norman's baggage, but not, thankfully, his clubs. So we were even lucky enough to be able to put him in a Kenmure shirt, with all three networks' affiliates having their camera crews dog Norman's every step — perfect.

Understandably, Norman's play was a little ragged at first. But on the inward half he played two strokes of genius that were well worth the price of admission. At the 196-yard fourteenth hole, played into the teeth of a freshening breeze, his towering four iron shot stopped no more than two inches from the hole, dead in the heart.

At the 399-yard eighteenth, a sharp dog leg to the right, Norman got full consent from the other three players to donate the $1,000 at stake there to the hospital, since Beck had already won $5,000 and the seniors each $3,500. Norman teed up his ball on a pencil and proceeded to drive over some singularly tall trees to the right to cut out the dog leg. His ball landed some 40 yards short of the green.

Although Greg was plainly exhausted — his European victory had been well celebrated — he gave ample time to the media, charmed the women and children at the subsequent cocktail party, and finally left for his Orlando home on the chartered jet in the shattering knowledge that he had to turn straight around and fly back to Scotland the next day for the Dunhill Cup at St. Andrews.

If anyone ever tries to tell me that Norman isn't a good and loyal friend, but just another spoiled millionaire, they will have a fierce argument on their hands.

In 1950 the U.S. PGA tour had a total prize money of $450,000. In 1991, 31 players on the PGA tour earned more than that.

For me, golf has been a 50-year-long love/hate relationship of endless fascination. It all started when my paternal grandfather, who was company secretary of the Triumph concern when it was alive and well and producing the finest-quality cars and motorcycles, gave me a mashie with a steel shaft that I suspect might have come off his machine shop floor. It was secured to the hosel by a substance that could have been chewing gum, putty, or even concrete. It mattered not at all to me that the shaft was totally inflexible. I learned quickly to use that extraordinary weapon with no little skill, and I was hooked on the game.

Today visitors to my home wonder at the colossal assortment of clubs that clutter more than one room and the garage, all of them rejects not because of their condition — most have barely been scarred — but because of my sorry inability to wield them with even minimal skill. I own no less than 58 drivers, all of them victims of a mental blockage that occurs whenever I pick up a wooden club, or the hated "Pittsburgh persimmon," with the number 1 on its sole plate. I suspect that any driver with even a seven-degree loft would suit me just perfectly, provided it had any other damned number on the bottom. Alas, I have finally settled on a Callaway Big Bertha with an 11-degree loft because it is so forgiving of my puny game.

For iron clubs I now vacillate between two matched sets of Ben Hogan Edges — the latest model — and the vastly different Cobra Baffler Blade II irons with the graphite Super Senior shafts.

When either set fails me — of course it is the clubs, not the man who does the failing — they are quickly relegated to the closet. But there are several more matched sets around if both fail me on a regular basis.

The tragedy of it all is that I played my best golf up to the age of 18 with an ill-assorted collection of unmatched, largely scruffy weapons. I was a fairly reliable two handicap on going to a war that never happened, and never was better than six thereafter. Now my handicap fluctuates between 10 and 14; if I play well I'm a sandbagger, and if I have a bad day my partner or fellow competitors rub salt into the wounds by telling me that what Gary McCord says about my game is absolutely correct.

Isn't it extraordinary that when one feels in the pink of condition, hits the ball beautifully on the practice tee, and bounds onto the first tee with unfettered enthusiasm for the game that the results are almost always disastrous? And just as surely when I have been out half the night, top or shank most of my few practice shots, and feel in imminent danger of collapse, my golf swing when I get to the first tee works like a well-oiled machine, or as near to that state of grace I am nowadays capable of achieving.

There is always a single decent shot or a snake of a no-brainer putt to bring me back for more cruel and unjust punishment. As the cliché goes, golf is an unfair game, but the good thing about it is that it is unfair to everybody.

My two holes in one typify the kind of golf of which I am capable. The first was recorded during my debut for the county of Bedfordshire, England, at the South Bedfordshire Golf Club on the northern outskirts of my hometown of Luton. I was a callow youth of 17 years, and because we were playing the hated rivals across the border from Hertfordshire, I was paired with the 13-times county champion, a veteran of such battles, in the bottom of our foursomes — Scotch foursomes as they are known here, or alternate shot foursomes.

We were two down with three holes to play on reaching a 127-yard sixteenth-

hole that was set on the side of a steep hill. The tee was carved out of the hill side, as was the narrow but deep green, which was fronted by two shallow bunkers. One walked in Indian file down a narrow pathway between tee and green. We were playing in a 20-miles-per-hour southwesterly wind, and our opponent was duly smug on hitting a lovely tee shot some four feet from the hole, particularly since it was I who was to hit the tee shot for our side.

I stone-cold topped that tee shot. The ball literally fizzed off my seven-iron in a series of frantic hops down the pathway. It veered a little right and fairly raced through the bunker, slammed against the flagstick, and dropped straight into the hole. We won the next two holes for good measure, and our beaten opponents refused to shake hands.

My second hole in one was achieved at Knollwood Country Club north of Chicago in the mid-1980s. We were playing what the organizer, my then CBS colleague Bob Drum, grandly titled "The CBS World Championship Two-Man Scramble." There were several professionals in the field, but yours truly was paired with a 16-handicap Milwaukee Bucks television announcer, and I was carrying, or rather dragging, a traveling 10 handicap at the time. I had contracted a bad case of food poisoning in Flint, Michigan, the previous weekend, and I gave Drum both barrels about the unfairness of our being paired in such a manner with no strokes against professionals. Needless to say, my protests fell on deaf ears, and away we went.

Luckily for me, the third hole at Knollwood returns to the clubhouse, because I was halfway down the third fairway when the remnant nausea of my food poisoning rushed up in my throat. I pushed my partner and his clubs out of the cart and told him to play the hole as well as he could alone, and I sped off. On returning to the fourth tee, I am told I cut a sorry figure, ashen faced and sweating profusely. Many rude words were spoken by a crowd of my fellow competitors waiting to play the fourth hole after us. I was indeed holding up play.

The hole measured 175 yards, and our caddy told me it was either a hard six or an easy five-iron. I replied tersely that the young man in question was obvious-ly not taking into account my physical condition, and I told him to give me the bloody four-iron. Of course, my only aim was not to fall over when hitting that tee shot, which bounced 15 feet in front of the hole, took a couple more hops, and ran quietly into the center of the hole to considerable and boisterous acclaim. My partner and I won the tournament with a 68 that contained but one bogey.

What I am really trying to say is that golf is endlessly fascinating to me because of its very unpredictability. I love it for the unfailingly beauty of its myriad settings I have been so privileged to enjoy all over the world, usually at other people's expense. I love it for its camaraderie and good fellowship. I only hate golf because, as far as skills are concerned, I am but a pale shadow of my former self as my shadow grows increasingly larger. But I can hardly wait to tee it up again this afternoon, regardless of the consequences,

which are increasingly disastrous with each passing year. What does it matter? I'll just drink in the fresh air, smell the flowers, and enjoy every crumb of comfort that I can grab from even the pitifully few shots I hit halfway decently.

But don't ever tell me it's only a game.

67. The 18th at St. Andrews, *Scotland*

Catalogue

Paintings are listed consecutively as they appear in the book. Sizes shown are in inches, with vertical measurements first.

1. Panorama at Turnberry
   6¹/₂ x 35¹/₄, watercolor

2. The Caddy
   14 x 12³/₈, watercolor

3. To the Tee
   14³/₄ x 10³/₈, watercolor

4. Off the 10th Tee
   12 x 18, oil

5. The Bell
   13 x 11³/₄, watercolor

6. Lining Up at Portmarnock
   12¹/₂ x 15¹/₂, watercolor

7. Hell Bunker at St. Andrews
   13¹/₂ x 23, watercolor

8. The Spectacles
   14¹/₂ x 26¹/₂, watercolor

9. Cart Reflections
   14¹/₂ x 9, watercolor

10. The Legendary Tree
    18 x 24, oil

11. Rough by the Sea
    14 x 24, watercolor

12. The 8th at Merion
    12¹/₂ x 18, watercolor

13. The Country Club
    18³/₄ x 24³/₄, watercolor

14. Checking In at Nairn
    10 x 15³/₄, watercolor

15. Oyster Reef
    17 x 28, watercolor

16. The Goats of Lahinch
    13³/₄ x 18¹/₂, watercolor

17. From the Rough
    17¹/₂ x 24¹/₂, watercolor

18. Ladies of the Club
    11¹/₂ x 23, watercolor

19. Playing through the Squall
    17¹/₂ x 24³/₈, watercolor

20. From the Trap at Royal Liverpool
    15¹/₂ x 20, watercolor

21. Over the Wall
    11 x 14, oil

22. Western Gailes
    10¹/₂ x 24¹/₂, watercolor

23. Sunningdale
    11¹/₂ x 17¹/₂, watercolor

24. Gleneagles
    12³/₄ x 13³/₄, watercolor

25. Mighty Cruden Bay
    14 x 21, watercolor

26. Reflections at Newport
    12 x 24³/₄, watercolor

27. A "Single" on Gullane #1
    13¹/₈ x 22¹/₈, watercolor

28. The Locker
    16¹/₄ x 10³/₄, watercolor

29. The "Postage Stamp" at Troon
    12¹/₂ x 20¹/₂, watercolor

30. Rain Gear
    11¹/₂ x 10¹/₂, watercolor

31. Royal Lytham
    12 x 18, oil

32. Going to the Co-op
    16 x 12, oil

33. Over the Gorse
    17¹/₂ x 24¹/₂, watercolor

34. Westport
    23 x 13¹/₂, watercolor

35. Checking the Distance
    17 x 24¹/₂, watercolor

36. Cypress Point
    17 x 28¹/₂, watercolor

37. The 4th at Baltusrol *
    19 x 20, watercolor

38. Shinnecock Hills Clubhouse
    13³/₄ x 32¹/₂, watercolor

39. The 6th at Seminole
    12 x 18, watercolor

40. The 18th at Harbour Town
    17¹/₂ x 17¹/₂, watercolor

41. The 15th at Harbour Town
    20 x 30, oil

42. The Wall at Dunbar
    13¹/₂ x 24¹/₂, watercolor

43. The Gin Game
    8¹/₂ x 13, watercolor

44. Practice Green at Augusta
    12 x 18, oil

45. Flagman at Augusta
    8 x 12, oil

46. Junior Golfer
    8¹/₂ x 7, watercolor

47. The Fabled 13th at Augusta
    16³/₄ x 29¹/₄, watercolor

48. The 10th at Muirfield
    13 x 21, watercolor

49. Laurie's Shop
    11³/₄ x 17³/₄, watercolor

50. Walking the Dog at Turnberry
    17¹/₄ x 19, watercolor

51. The Church Pews
    16 x 25, watercolor

52. Trap by the Windmill
    11⁵/₈ x 17³/₈, watercolor

53. Working Together
    14 x 13, watercolor

54. The Stout Drinker
    10 x 6, watercolor

55. The Maintenance Shack
    11 x 17¹/₂, watercolor

56. The Awesome 17th at Kiawah
    20 x 30, oil

57. Pinehurst #2
    12 x 18, oil

58. Spring Foursome
    16¹/₂ x 25, watercolor

59. The 17th at Medina
    10¹/₂ x 12¹/₂, watercolor

60. Pebble Beach
    18 x 24, oil

61. The 5th at Pine Valley
    19¹/₂ x 20³/₈, watercolor

62. Basket Flag at Merion
    11 x 13, watercolor

63. A Testing 3 at Royal Birkdale
    11 x 24¹/₂, watercolor

64. Clubhouse at Medina
    9 x 9, watercolor

65. The Approach at Shinnecock Hills
    12 x 18, oil

66. TPC Sawgrass
    16³/₄ x 25, watercolor

67. The 18th at St. Andrews
    15¹/₂ x 25¹/₂, watercolor

All paintings are the property of
Ray Ellis Gallery
205 West Congress Street
Savannah, Georgia 31401
* Private collection

Good golf is a state of mind

Golf is deceptively simple, and endlessly complicated. A child can play it well, and a grown man can never master it. Any single round of it is full of unexpected triumphs and seemingly perfect shots that end in disaster.

It is almost a science, yet it is a puzzle without an answer. It is gratifying and tantalizing, precise and unpredictable. It requires complete concentration and total relaxation. It satisfies the soul and frustrates the intellect.

It is at the same time rewarding and maddening – and it is without doubt the greatest game mankind has ever invented.

One of today's most highly regarded impressionist painters, **Ray Ellis** is perhaps best known for the three best-selling books on which he collaborated with Walter Cronkite: *South by Southeast, North by Northeast*, and *Westwind*.

Ben Wright, often referred to as "The Voice of Golf," has been a CBS golf analyst for nearly twenty years. His writing on the sport has appeared in countless periodicals throughout the United States and Europe.

John deGarmo, who conceived the idea for *The Spirit of Golf*, spent more than thirty years in the advertising business in New York. His fascination with Hasselblad, one of his accounts, led to a love of photography. All of the photographs in this book are his, and many of Ray Ellis's paintings were inspired by them. DeGarmo also has a mid single-digit handicap and was Advisory Board Chairman of The American Junior Golf Association.